Cambridge Elements

Elements in Comparative Political Behavior
edited by
Raymond Duch
University of Oxford
Anja Neundorf
University of Glasgow
Randy Stevenson
Rice University

VOTERS' PERCEPTIONS OF PARTY BRANDS

David Fortunato
University of California, San Diego

Thiago N. Silva
The Australian National University

Laron K. Williams
University of Missouri

Shaftesbury Road, Cambridge CB2 8EA, United Kingdom

One Liberty Plaza, 20th Floor, New York, NY 10006, USA

477 Williamstown Road, Port Melbourne, VIC 3207, Australia

314–321, 3rd Floor, Plot 3, Splendor Forum, Jasola District Centre,
New Delhi – 110025, India

103 Penang Road, #05–06/07, Visioncrest Commercial, Singapore 238467

Cambridge University Press is part of Cambridge University Press & Assessment,
a department of the University of Cambridge.

We share the University's mission to contribute to society through the pursuit of
education, learning and research at the highest international levels of excellence.

www.cambridge.org
Information on this title: www.cambridge.org/9781009644365

DOI: 10.1017/9781009417792

© David Fortunato, Thiago N. Silva, and Laron K. Williams 2025

This publication is in copyright. Subject to statutory exception and to the provisions
of relevant collective licensing agreements, no reproduction of any part may take
place without the written permission of Cambridge University Press & Assessment.

When citing this work, please include a reference to the DOI 10.1017/9781009417792

First published 2025

A catalogue record for this publication is available from the British Library

ISBN 978-1-009-64436-5 Hardback
ISBN 978-1-009-41780-8 Paperback
ISSN 2754-6144 (online)
ISSN 2754-6136 (print)

Additional resources for this publication at www.cambridge.org/fortunato-et-al

Cambridge University Press & Assessment has no responsibility for the persistence
or accuracy of URLs for external or third-party internet websites referred to in this
publication and does not guarantee that any content on such websites is, or will
remain, accurate or appropriate.

For EU product safety concerns, contact us at Calle de José Abascal, 56, 1°, 28003
Madrid, Spain, or email eugpsr@cambridge.org

Voters' Perceptions of Party Brands

Elements in Comparative Political Behavior

DOI: 10.1017/9781009417792
First published online: August 2025

David Fortunato
University of California, San Diego

Thiago N. Silva
The Australian National University

Laron K. Williams
University of Missouri

Author for correspondence: David Fortunato, dfortunato@ucsd.edu

Abstract: In order to cast a satisfying vote, understand politics, or otherwise participate in political discourse or processes, voters must have some idea of what policies parties are pursuing and, more generally, "who goes with whom." This Element aims to both advance the study of how voters formulate and update their perceptions of party brands and persuade our colleagues to join us in studying these processes. To make this endeavor more enticing, but no less rigorous, we make three contributions to this emerging field of study: presenting a framework for building and interrogating theoretical arguments, aggregating a large, comprehensive data archive, and recommending a parsimonious strategy for statistical analysis. In the process, we provide a definition for voters' perceptions of party brands and an analytical schema to study them, attempt to contextualize and rationalize some competing findings in the existing literature, and derive and test several new hypotheses.

Keywords: coalition, coalition politics, comparative politics, democratic responsiveness, elections, electoral competition, electoral politics, European politics, party politics, political behavior, political knowledge

© David Fortunato, Thiago N. Silva, and Laron K. Williams 2025

ISBNs: 9781009644365 (HB), 9781009417808 (PB), 9781009417792 (OC)
ISSNs: 2754-6144 (online), 2754-6136 (print)

Contents

1 Why Study Voters' Perceptions of Party Brands?   1
2 Building a Theoretical Argument   17
3 Data, Measurement of Perceptions, and
   Modeling Choices   28
4 Putting It All Together   56
5 Where to Go from Here   69

   References   78

1 Why Study Voters' Perceptions of Party Brands?

Learning how voters understand the menu of options before them is pivotal to the study of representative democracy. The possession of relatively accurate and up-to-date perceptions of the policies parties are likely to favor and pursue is integral to understanding policymaking and policy outcomes as well as generating reasonable expectations of the policy consequences of one's vote, or aggregate electoral outcomes, and is therefore necessary for prospective selection of representatives and the issuance of policy mandates. If voters do not have a reasonable understanding of which policies parties are likely to pursue, then they will not be able to find a reasonable match at the ballot box and cannot hope to channel their policy preferences into policy outcomes. As such, representative democracy as understood by modern political scientists cannot properly function if voters are not attuned and responsive to the policy ambitions of the parties competing to represent them. Indeed, as we explain later, voters' perceptions of parties' policy goals do not just *facilitate* the democratic processes that shape policy outcomes; they *animate* them.

We have written this Element to encourage you, our colleague, to study these perceptions, precisely because we believe they are integral to countless choices and cognitions made by voters, and, as a result, integral to democratic processes in theory and in fact. To encourage you, we use this section to briefly summarize why these perceptions are important and how they shape political processes and outcomes in representative democracies. We then explain three opportunities presented by the extant literature to make studying these perceptions easier, but no less rigorous, and hopefully hasten and expand our aggregate understanding of how party perceptions are formed, updated, and employed. We close with the plan of this Element.

1.1 Making Political Inferences and Choices

Understanding political processes, particularly multiparty policymaking, requires an understanding of "who wants what" and "who goes with whom."[1] Making sense of policymaking processes like the formation of governing coalitions, distribution of leadership roles, and votes over legislative proposals requires understanding what parties' goals are and which parties are compatible. Fortunato, Stevenson, and Vonnahme (2016, 1212) define three basic "functions of partisan left-right metaphor" for accomplishing this task.

---

[1] Of course, parties also need to forge majorities within their ranks, particularly in imperfectly disciplined, single-member systems.

The first is to summarize policy positions over a broad array of individual jurisdictions. This allows voters to substitute a party's general position for a larger number of specific positions on distinct dimensions in order to reduce the effort of organizing the political landscape and finding the parties offering the most compatible policies.[2] The second function is to guide "affective orientations" (Dalton 2014) – which may be driven by policy but can also be borne out of socialization or salient cultural considerations (Huddy, Mason, and Aarøe 2015) – and the sorting of parties into "left" and "right" groups to provide a shortcut for intuiting which parties are and are not acceptable alternatives. The third function is to map the relative compatibility of parties in order to understand the formation, maintenance, and change of policymaking coalitions. These three functions are *not* mutually exclusive.

It is fairly clear how each of these functions maps onto political behavior. If voters are what Cox (1997) would call *sincere*, then policy summaries or affective orientations alone are sufficient to make a satisfying choice. If voters take into account postelectoral bargaining, as argued by Gschwend (2001), Kedar (2005), and Duch, May, and Armstrong (2010), then voters would rely upon the third function to infer which coalitions were likely or unlikely and forecast their probable policy output. Even if voters are purely retrospective (rather than prospective) in their choices, possessing some sense of which party constellations are and are not compatible is integral to coordinating on viable alternatives to the incumbent.

Perhaps even more importantly, being able to array the parties in the policy space allows voters to understand who goes with whom in the most general terms. Understanding compatibility is essential not only for inferring which coalition cabinets may or may not form, but also for making sense of more general patterns of conflict and cooperation. This is necessary for interpreting discrete political events in the broader political landscape and for being able to discuss politics in a reasonably coherent fashion. Of course, the institutional context will determine how party positions may be aggregated or contrasted and for what purposes, but the central point of this discussion is that possessing relatively accurate perceptions of where the parties are in some policy space is a necessary condition for meaningful political participation in nearly all democratic systems.

---

[2] This organization also allows voters to make reasonably accurate inferences about a party's specific policy position on a specific jurisdiction, provided they are able to orient that specific issue to the general space.

1.2 Animating Partisan Behavior

Coarsening to a single point in a single jurisdiction, we can think of every party as having (at least) three policy positions. The first is its "true" position, or its actual, sincere policy intentions. The second is its strategically selected, advertised position, or what the party *wishes voters to believe* its policy intentions are for the purpose of maximizing votes. The third is the voters' perception of the party position, which is what will ultimately drive voters' behavior and therefore electoral returns.

Given that voters' perceptions of parties' brands are integral to their vote choices, parties have substantial incentive to ensure that voters perceive them as they *wish to be* perceived. To date, there is a comparatively large amount of research on how preferences in the electorate may motivate parties to update their policy offerings (e.g., Somer-Topcu 2009; Schumacher, De Vries, and Vis 2013; Klüver and Spoon 2016) and the findings are generally positive, suggesting that parties strategically adjust their policy offerings in response to the changing demands of the electorate in general or certain subgroups, notably their core supporters.

But what voters want from parties is not the only concern. How voters *perceive* parties to be positioned is critical as well. If parties have staked out some position in order to appeal to voters, deviations in voters' perception of that position can be electorally costly. As such, parties are incentivized to take all kinds of actions, apart from simply adjusting their manifestos, to try to manipulate voters' perceptions. Some of these actions may be relatively costless signaling, like issuing a press release (Sagarzazu and Klüver 2017) or engaging in prime ministerial debates (Sagarzazu and Williams 2017), but others may have fairly profound policy implications, as discussed in detail by Fortunato (2021). Though this research is nascent, the early efforts imply that voters' perceptions incentivize parties to take fairly drastic actions (e.g., Somer-Topcu 2017; O'Brien 2019; Somer-Topcu, Tavits, and Baumann 2020), such that any comprehensive understanding of party politics will require theoretical incorporation of voters' perceptions of the parties.

1.3 State of the Literature and Opportunities for Growth

Theoretical and empirical research on party politics is thriving in political science. We see this research defined by three overlapping foci. The first is concerned with the institutional foundations of party systems and the strategic origins of party entry and positioning. The second explores whether and how party positioning responds to changing voter preferences. The third, our focus

Table 1 Two foundational questions and conflicting answers

Question: *Do voters perceive party policy shifts?*

Source	Answer
Seeberg, Slothuus, and Stubager (2017)	Yes
Fernandez-Vazquez (2014)	Small effect
Plescia and Staniek (2017)	Conditional on issues
Adams, Ezrow, and Wlezien (2016)	No
Adams, Ezrow, and Somer-Topcu (2014)	Perhaps negatively

Question: *Do voters react to shifts in parties' policy positions?*

Source	Answer
Somer-Topcu (2015)	Yes
Bawn and Somer-Topcu (2012)	Conditional on government status
Tavits (2007)	Conditional on issues
Adams et al. (2006)	Only niche parties
Adams, Bernardi, and Wlezien (2020)	No

here, examines voters' responses to changes in the competitive environment, including party programs, government formation, party leadership, and other partisan choices inside and outside of the policymaking process.

The first two literatures have come to a relative consensus on basic conclusions to which we are continually adding nuance – that is, permissive electoral institutions create a diffuse set of parties advocating a wide range of policies (e.g., Cox 1990; Adams and Merril III 1999; Meguid 2005), and these parties are generally responsive to changes in the electorate's preferences (e.g., Somer-Topcu 2009; Van Der Velden, Schumacher, and Vis 2018; Weeks et al. 2023). The third literature, our focus here, has yet to reach empirical consensus, and could be fairly described as a series of competing results on some of its most basic questions.

Table 1 demonstrates some of the variability in previous empirical results by tabulating the answers to two core questions. The first is: Do voters perceive the changes parties make to their policy platforms? The literature here analyzes voters' perceptions of party brands, or locations in the policy space, and asks whether changes in the parties' policy goals, as manifest in campaign platforms, trigger the expected (i.e., positive) changes in how voters perceive the parties. The selection of findings in Table 1 shows that the answers vary widely. Existing research finds the expected positive effects, null effects, and even negative correlations between platform changes and changes in perceptions.

Answers to the second question are similarly varied: Do voters adjust their behavior in response to platform changes? Table 1 shows answers from studies asking whether voters are responsive to changes in party programs by examining changes in their own self-positioning or voting behavior. Again, answers vary widely from a fairly unequivocal "yes" to a fairly unequivocal "no." The wide-ranging answers to these two basic questions stand in stark comparison to the theoretical and normative consensus that the answer *should* be a resounding "yes."

Given theoretical consensus that the relationship should be positive, the finding that "[t]here is only weak and inconsistent empirical evidence that citizens in multiparty systems systematically react to parties' policy shifts" (Adams, De Vries, and Leiter 2012, 412), is paradoxical. Indeed, this inconsistency is sufficiently well understood that recent articles, for example, by Plescia and Staniek (2017), Seeberg, Slothuus, and Stubager (2017), and Adams, Bernardi, and Wlezien (2020), have taken to using it as a central motivator for their studies – and with good reason. It is vexing to review the literature on fairly fundamental questions of democratic responsiveness and find such varied results. What may explain this inconsistency? In this section, we contend that the lack of agreement is attributable to three central sources: theoretical foundations, small and inconsistent data, and empirical modeling strategies.

1.4 Theoretical Foundations

Part of the instability in past findings arises from a lack of a shared theoretical framework for investigating how voters form their perceptions of party policy positions and why and how these perceptions may change over time. As a point of contrast, the spatial model is the heart and soul of theoretical research in party politics, particularly the literature on strategic entry and positioning. But the consensus that we see regarding the spatial model as the theoretical foundation of research on parties' strategic entry and positioning is simply absent from research on how voters perceive parties' programs. The lack of consensus on a theoretical framework is evident in the text discussing basic assumptions about parties and voters and also in the structure of empirical models, particularly in observational studies. That is, theoretical frameworks lay the foundation for empirical models and, because theoretical perspectives on how voters form and update their party perceptions vary widely from study to study, the empirical research on the link between party policy signaling and voter perceptions of parties' policy positions (or aggregate party support) appears to lack institutional memory. As a result, the consensus and accumulation of knowledge that is typically reflected in the stability of included covariates in empirical models of other durable questions in political economic research is still lacking in this literature.

As another point of comparison, consider the literature on conflict. Fearon (1995) breathed new life into the bargaining theory of war (typically traced back to Schelling 1960), which was subsequently adopted as the core theoretical foundation of conflict research through at least 2010 (e.g., Walter 1997; Slantchev 2003; Little and Zeitzoff 2017). As a result, there has been for some time relative consensus amongst theorists and empiricists that conflict in general can be represented as a bargaining process and wars can be represented as inefficient attempts at resolution, typically brought about by "informational problems, bargaining indivisibilities, and commitment issues" (Powell 2006, 169–170). Because these scholars generally agree on first principles – what wars are and how or why wars start – they have a common language, make common assumptions, and scrutinize their theoretical arguments on common grounds. This agreement on theoretical foundations leads to agreement over the construction of empirical models. It would be odd to see a statistical model of war onset that lacked covariates capturing states' relative capabilities. Conversely, a reader can observe a significant level of variation in the included covariates when comparing studies on the implications of party-policy shifts. We believe that emerging studies, including this one, face steep challenges in establishing overarching theoretical arguments or common theoretical frameworks, which, in turn, lead to challenges establishing consistent empirical model strategies.

Because empirical models are borne of theoretical arguments, we can get a tangible sense of the variability in theoretical approaches with data by comparing several recent articles we feel are of a high quality and representative of the broader literature after surveying four prestigious, general political science journals.[3] Almost every empirical model specification in this literature takes the following form: The outcome is a measure of either voters' perceptions of a party's ideological position or a party's vote share; the central predictor is a measure of party policy position or position change over time, typically derived from manifesto codings or expert survey.[4] The similarities, however, tend to end there. We illustrate this with just three core covariates in Table 2.

---

[3] The list of articles included and their respective samples can be seen in Table A1 and Table A2 of the Supplementary Material (available online at www.cambridge.org/fortunato-et-al).

[4] This consistency aids in making our selected studies comparable and in identifying their differences despite their similar foundational empirical model specification.

Table 2 Meta-analysis of studies

Study ID	Reference	Lagged DV	Party appeal	Governing status
1	Adams et al. (2006)	✓	✓	✗
2	Adams, Ezrow, and Somer-Topcu (2011)	✓	✗	✗
3	Bawn and Somer-Topcu (2012)	✓	✓	✓
4	Fortunato and Stevenson (2013a)	✗	✓	✓
5	Schumacher, De Vries, and Vis (2013)	✗	✗	✗
6	Adams, Ezrow, and Somer-Topcu (2014)	✗	✗	✗
7	Ezrow, Homola, and Tavits (2014)	✗	✓	✗
8	Ezrow, Tavits, and Homola (2014)	✗	✓	✗
9	Fernandez-Vazquez (2014)*	✓	✗	✗
10	Dalton and McAllister (2015)	✗	✓	✓
11	Somer-Topcu (2015)	✓	✓	✓
12	Adams, Ezrow, and Wlezien (2016)	✗	✗	✓
13	Fernandez-Vazquez and Somer-Topcu (2019)	✓	✗	✓
14	Adams, Weschle, and Wlezien (2021)	✗	✗	✓

Notes: *Lagged DV* indicates the inclusion of a lagged dependent variable as a covariate on the model specification.

Party appeal indicates the inclusion of a covariate to distinguish between "niche" and "mainstream" parties in the model specification. As niche parties often adopt more radical or extreme ideologies, we also considered studies that either explain the variability of electoral support for extreme parties (Ezrow, Homola, and Tavits 2014; Ezrow, Tavits, and Homola 2014) or include a control for the parties' level of extremism (Bawn and Somer-Topcu 2012; Fortunato and Stevenson 2013a) or moderation (Somer-Topcu 2015) as fulfilling this condition.

Governing status indicates the inclusion of a covariate in the model specification to distinguish between political parties that are part of the government (i.e., parties that hold a position in the executive cabinet or are members of the coalition government) and those in the opposition (i.e., parties that do not hold positions in the executive cabinet and do not support the government in parliament).

*Fernandez-Vazquez (2014) transforms the first-differences model strategy proposed by Adams, Ezrow, and Somer-Topcu (2011) into a model in levels.

Table 2 shows that some studies include a lagged dependent variable, while others do not, despite evidence that a lagged dependent ("Lagged DV" in the table) variable is important (Fernandez-Vazquez 2014). Some studies differentiate between "niche" and "mainstream" parties, or account in some way for parties' extremism ("Party appeal"), but most pool these observations, despite evidence that these parties face differing electoral incentives (Adams et al. 2006). Similarly, some studies incorporate information on the governing status of parties ("Governing status"), but most do not, despite evidence that it is critical (Bawn and Somer-Topcu 2012).

We contend that a central reason for the substantial variability in empirical models of voter perceptions (or responses more broadly) is the absence of a common theoretical framework that can guide the development of empirical strategies. Whereas conflict scholars have generally come to agreement over what wars are and how or why wars start, we have yet to come to such an agreement over what party perceptions are and how or why they change. In the absence of such a framework, we do not have a common language and thus we cannot make common assumptions or scrutinize theoretical arguments on common grounds. As a result, we may inadvertently overlook pertinent covariates when constructing empirical models, potentially leading to omitted variable bias or contributing to relatively low levels of model fit or efficiency. This makes cross-study comparisons challenging.

To address this, we propose a theoretical framework in Section 2, inspired by Fiorina (1981) and Zaller (1992), that gives a fairly formal definition of what voters' perceptions of parties are and how or why they change, as well as a clear, rigorous, but still simple process to scrutinize theoretical arguments about specific factors that may change them.

1.5 Small or Inconsistent Data

Most studies in this literature focus on the party-time period as the unit of observation, asking whether or how voters' perceptions of parties have changed, in the aggregate, and why. The unit of observation tends toward the party election because the focus of study is nearly always on party- or party-election-level characteristics, most often changes in party policy commitments, cabinet participation, etc. Each election, or election survey, therefore yields just as many observations as there are (relevant) parties. As a result, aggregate sample size tends to be small, normally in the range of about 100 and nearly always less than 200. By itself, small samples need not perturb analyses, particularly if the universe of relevant events is itself small. But that is not necessarily the case here, as there have been many democratic elections in the years since electoral surveying has become common place. Consequently, the small (on average) sample sizes have led to a striking degree of variability in the sample of survey-years used to analyze voter perceptions.

This sample variability is illustrated in Figure 1, which is based on the articles listed in Table 2 and data for European countries from 1969 to 2019.[5] In Figure 1, each row corresponds to a country, and the shading reflects the number of articles using the same country-year observations. Darker shading indicates a higher degree of sample overlap among the studies. The countries are ordered based on the total count of country-year observations, with the Netherlands being the most commonly studied, followed by Germany, while Eastern European countries (Ukraine, Russia, Croatia, Bulgaria, and Albania) are the least commonly studied.[6] In the following text, we illustrate the sample variability with specific examples from these high-quality, well-cited articles. Before doing so, it is important to note several factors that may contribute to the samples used in these articles – limitations on core covariates apart from voter perceptions, institutional or temporal factors that are critical to the study context, etc. We do not mean to imply that for one study or another to not include a particular observation is indicative of a lesser quality, only that, in the aggregate, lower levels of observational overlap across studies may drive variance in empirical conclusions.

The heat map reveals significant variation in the samples used by different studies in terms of both countries covered and temporal coverage. To get a more tangible grasp on this variability, we compare some studies that utilize the same dependent variable – the mean voter-perceived position of a particular party derived from a specific electoral survey. Falcó-Gimeno and Fernandez-Vazquez (2020) examine the impact of coalition participation on voter perceptions in Denmark, Germany, the Netherlands, Norway, and Sweden, utilizing a sample that includes surveys conducted over an average of 7.6 different years. Fernandez-Vazquez (2014) adds the United Kingdom to this sample in his examination of the durability of party perceptions in the face of changing programs, and the average number of survey-years per country stays roughly equivalent. Fernandez-Vazquez and Somer-Topcu (2019) add Spain to that updated sample in their investigation of the impact of changes in party leadership to voter perceptions, and again the average number of survey-years per country stays roughly equivalent. To analyze the application of coalition participation heuristics on voter perceptions of parties' positions on EU integration, Adams, Ezrow, and Wlezien (2016) use

---

[5] To ensure consistency with the data coverage, the article by Adams et al. (2006) was excluded from the analysis due to its publication date.

[6] The sample variability across studies can be seen in Table A2 of the Supplementary Material (available online at www.cambridge.org/fortunato-et-al).

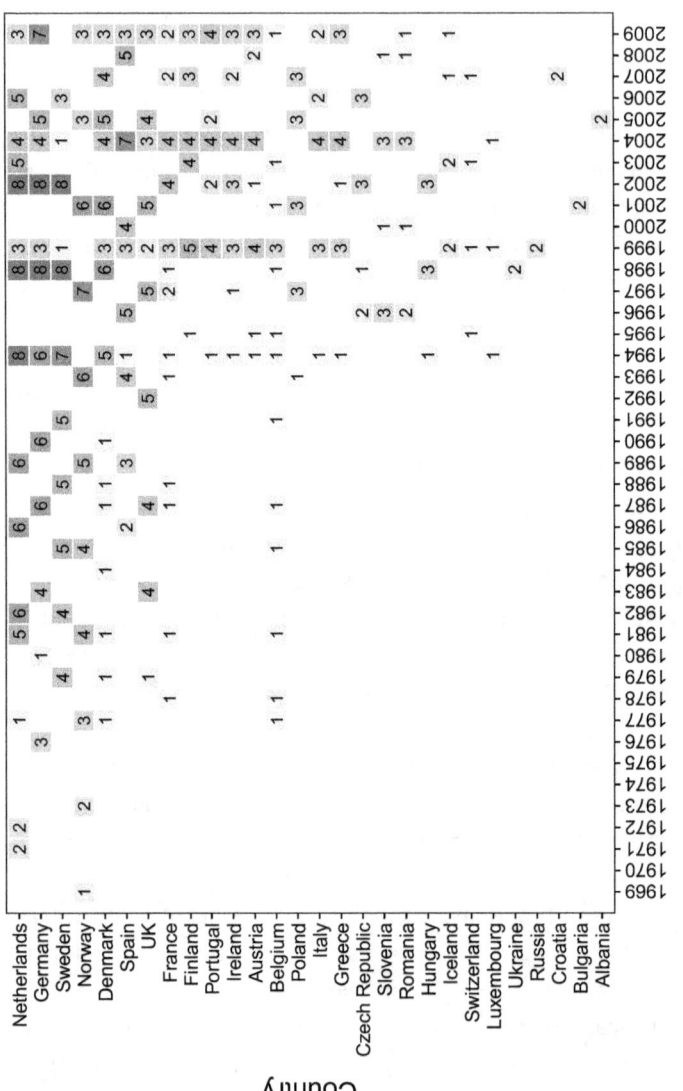

Figure 1 Number of studies using the same country-year observations.

Note: keeping only articles published after 2010, and data covering European countries from 1969 to 2009

a sample of three survey-years for eight countries: Austria, Denmark, Finland, Germany, Ireland, Italy, the Netherlands, and Portugal; only three of which overlap the countries in Fernandez-Vazquez and Somer-Topcu (2019). Ezrow, Homola, and Tavits (2014), in turn, present a sample of 32 countries, with an average of about two survey-years each, to examine the variability of voter perceptions of partisan policy positions.

We demonstrate the sample variability more rigorously by calculating a summary measure of the overlap. We begin by identifying all unique (unordered) study pairs.[7] For each dyad, we calculate the total number of country-years appearing in the analyses (agnostic over which parties are studied within any country-year) and the number of *intersecting* country-years – the observations that appear in both studies in the dyad. Summing all intersecting country-year counts and dividing by total country-year counts reveals that the total empirical overlap across all studies is 14.37%. That is, for any given study, only 14.37% of its analyzed country-years will also appear in another given study on average. It is no surprise, then, that there is a large degree of inconsistency in empirical results across studies.

Importantly, however, sample variability need not be detrimental for scientific progress. In fact, testing a theory's predictions in different contexts is instrumental. But this variability is not driven by scholars searching for new contexts to test their theoretical predictions. These are all studies focused on modern, wealthy, predominantly Western European democracies. This means that deviations from the universe of available data on these democracies are likely just depriving researchers of analytical power, potentially hindering their ability to discover hypothesized relationships.

So what drives the instability? As mentioned, there are likely several practical concerns that create differing limitations on the cases being studied: institutional factors, temporal factors, lack of overlap on important covariates, and so on. But we believe that the core factor is data availability, or accessibility. While our colleagues studying conflict have access to databases such as the Correlates of War and Militarized Interstate Disputes, which provide a relatively complete account of events, we currently lack such a comprehensive resource.

To address the issue of sample variability, in Section 3 we present Sophia: The Party Perceptions Data, a dataset aggregating all parliamentary electoral surveys contained in all modules of three cooperative cross-national surveying projects: the European Voter Project (EVP), the European Election Studies (EES), and the Comparative Study of Electoral Systems (CSES). We also

---

[7] This is a 14 choose 2 problem ($_{n=14}C_{r=2}$), yielding 91 study dyads.

added several national election studies not included in EVP or CSES to fill in some gaps. As described in more detail in Section 3, Sophia contains voter perceptions of 458 parties across 38 countries and spanning 54 years (from 1965 to 2019), derived from 321 surveys. This yields 1,988 total party-time observations. Of course, several parties only appear once, but others appear a dozen times or more (our final dynamic estimation sample, after restricting the sample to parliamentary systems, includes 1,732 observations).

1.6 Empirical Strategies

Recall our argument that the variability in specifications – that is, which predictors are included on the right-hand side of the equation when modeling voter perceptions – is at least partially a function of the diffuse nature of the theoretical approaches to the question. There are also certain estimation habits, however, that we believe may be contributing to the instability in empirical results, and we discuss three in particular here. The first is the use of raw survey means of voters' ideological placements of parties as the dependent variable; the second is the lack of consideration of measurement error in both dependent and independent variables; the third is the dynamic structure of the statistical model.

Survey means are the industry standard dependent variable in the literature on voters' perceptions of parties. Survey respondents are asked to place parties on an ideological continuum, typically from 0 to 10, or another similar scale, where small values correspond to left-leaning preferences (e.g., high taxation and public goods provision) and high values correspond to right-leaning preferences (e.g., low taxation and public goods provision). Analysts then average all respondent placements of the parties being analyzed and use this average as the general measure of how voters perceive those parties' ideological positions. This is intuitive for both the analyst and the reader, efficient, and easily reproducible – three highly valued criteria in scientific research. However, we see this approach as having (at least) three salient drawbacks.

The first drawback is that there is a high degree of variability in *who* places the parties. That is, survey respondents will often choose not to offer an estimate of a party's ideological position for any number of reasons, but we suspect that the primary reason is a lack of familiarity with the party. Indeed, Ezrow, Homola, and Tavits (2014) find a very strong correlation between the proportion of respondents that place a party and its size. This correlation suggests that we may obtain systematically "better" or "more accurate" placements of *smaller* parties because only respondents with relatively high levels of political interest are offering placements for them. The fact that ideologically extreme parties tend to be smaller suggests a systematic correspondence between mean placements and parties' policy programs – the most common independent variable in this literature – creating substantial potential confounding. This is just one possibility, of course, and one could imagine other biases potentially being injected into our models as a result of nonresponse (e.g., Fortunato et al. 2024).

The second issue is closely related. If we take the mean of all placements, then we are aggregating the placements of very different kinds of respondents in a uniform manner. For instance, we are combining the placements of individuals who are young and may have recently started paying attention to politics and forming their perceptions of these parties' positions, with those who are older and may have formed their perceptions decades ago and not updated them since. We are also aggregating the perceptions of party members or supporters, who presumably have a better idea of what their party stands for, with those of nonsupporters, who may have comparably less reliable information. This is particularly relevant because the mix of supporters and nonsupporters varies systematically across parties and countries.

The third issue with survey means is the strong assumptions required for comparability. If we compare the mean placement of the United Kingdom's Labour Party in 2010 to its mean placement in 2015, we assume that the sample of respondents in 2010 is, if not identical to, sufficiently representative of the sample of respondents in 2015 to ignore the possibility of differences in placements as a function of the sample demographics. At first blush, this is not an unreasonable assumption. After all, electoral surveys are specifically designed to be representative of the voting population and survey administrators take great pains to calculate and include a set of respondent weights to achieve this representativeness. But these weights are rarely employed, and, if they are used, they are almost never mentioned in the text of these articles. Further, when we consider the variability in sample sizes and nonresponse (which are not taken into account in sample weights), these assumptions begin to feel less tenable. For example, the European Election Studies, an invaluable resource to this literature, surveyed about 1,100 residents of each EU member state in 2014. Given that the weights tend to be ignored, we are likely to have a much better sample of 2014 Estonia, a country of about 1 million, than 2014 France, a country of about 66 million. Moreover, there is likely to be systematic variation across these countries in the extent to which the assumptions required for comparing averages hold both *within* countries and *across* survey iterations.

Our second critique of the typical approach to empirical modeling is a reiteration of Benoit, Laver, and Mikhaylov (2009): Extant studies nearly always ignore measurement error in both the dependent and independent variables. We believe that this is almost certainly a function of the lag between this research's beginnings and the revelation of how critical it is to model errors in the focal variables – for example, party policy placements derived from campaign manifestos, electoral surveys, expert evaluations, etc. Nonetheless, the literature has now slain those dragons and strategies for estimating variance in manifesto-derived positions (Benoit, Laver, and Mikhaylov 2009; Lowe et al. 2011) or expert surveys (Lindstädt, Proksch, and Slapin 2016) are now available. In short, particularly in light of what we learned through Benoit, Laver, and Mikhaylov's (2009) replication exercise, we cannot continue to ignore the reality that the key covariates in this literature are estimated with error.

Finally, approaches to dynamic modeling vary substantially across studies. Recall the variation in inclusion of a lagged dependent variable in Table 2: About half of the studies included a lagged DV and about half did not. Variability in the structure of the predictor variables – whether researchers use only concurrent values, lagged values, change in value, or some combination of the three – is even broader. As we discuss later, these differences are critical, not only for comparability of model results, but, more importantly, because the model's dynamic structure imposes strict assumptions on the theoretical data-generating process. More specifically, some relationships that may in fact be in the data are restricted to zero by assumption, causing potential spillover into the estimated covariance of correlated variables. We present a simple empirical specification that is sufficiently flexible to be considered a "one-size-fits-all" approach for nearly all applications.

In the remainder of this Element, we provide potential solutions to the three potential sources of discord outlined in Section 1. First, we develop a theoretical framework to understand the formulation and updating of voters' perceptions of party positions. Second, we present the aggregation of many electoral surveys, which we have harmonized and imputed for missingness. Third, we derive a new, more stable estimate of aggregate voter perceptions, discuss its error properties, and present a simple, one-size-fits-all dynamic model structure, with instructions for refitting it to different theoretical conceptions of the data-generating process (if need be). The goal, as we noted, is to make studying voters' perceptions more enticing. We wish to give the field a small set of common assumptions and a language to derive and scrutinize hypotheses, as well as a large, common data archive and a simple modeling framework with which we may test those hypotheses.

1.7 Plan of This Element

To make it more enticing to explore these questions, we wish to provide something of a "starter kit" for future research. In Section 2, we describe a framework for constructing and scrutinizing theoretical arguments regarding voter perceptions of party brands, inspired by Fiorina (1981) and Zaller (1992). A key insight is that we should consider voters' perceptions of parties' distributions, rather than points. The framework is simple and parsimonious, providing a foundation for understanding how voters' perceptions change by considering the *cost*, *credibility*, and *salience* (CCS) of information connoting partisan preferences. After presenting this framework – which we call the CCS framework – we illustrate its utility by revisiting previous research that can be organized and synthesized in its context before applying it to two well-researched predictors of voters' perceptions – government composition and campaign manifestos. A central feature of the framework (apart from its simplicity and flexibility) is that it bears clear implications for empirical strategies to modeling both the mean *and* variance of voters' perceptions of party positions. We return to this feature in Section 4.

In Section 3, we present the comprehensive new data on voter perceptions (Sophia), and then argue for a new measure of voter perceptions. The data are composed of more than 3 million responses to 321 surveys, administered across 38 countries, covering 458 different parties. Our new measure is motivated by a discussion of potential issues with the present industry standard (the unweighted, survey mean perception) and constructed to meet these challenges. We simply predict how all parties would be perceived by an identical respondent, which we model as the global mode of the full sample – the package of values that collectively occur most frequently in the data. This is a 40-year-old woman with a secondary education, median self-placement, and middle-class income who does not identify with the party she is evaluating. We call these estimates "Sophia," the most common woman's name in Europe, which means *wisdom* in Greek, making it an appropriate name for an estimate of party placements based on the wisdom of crowds.[8] In scrutinizing the measurement, we show that its face validity, appropriateness for dynamic estimation, and error properties are preferable to the (unweighted) sample mean.

In Section 3, we make the case for using an *Autoregressive Distributed Lag* (ADL) specification for modeling voters' perceptions. Key to this case is

---

[8] We thank Debra Leiter for pointing out this happy coincidence.

flexibility: A fully specified ADL model allows the manifestation of current and lagged short- and long-term effects of covariates on the outcome, whereas several other specifications used in previous research constrain certain effects to zero by omitting lagged or concurrent values of covariates. We present this simply, with substantive illustrations and graphics, in addition to the requisite mathematical notation. The key point we want readers to take away from this section is that empirical specifications formalize unbreakable theoretical assumptions and lock them into the estimation process, constraining the range of relationships allowed to manifest.

In Section 4, we apply the theoretical framework described in Section 2 to make an argument about how the mean and variance of voters' perceptions of government and opposition parties should respond to their campaign platforms, governance status, and electoral context. We then use the data we have gathered to estimate the empirical model implied by the argument and interpret our findings.

We find that voters' perceptions of the parties' policy stands are remarkably stable, but do, in fact, change in response to government formation and alterations to policy programs. More specifically, we demonstrate that voters tend to "push" coalition partners together and "pull" opposition parties away from the cabinet. While previous research has found that voters perceive coalition partners as more similar, the finding that voters pull opposition parties away from the cabinet is novel. Our analysis also reveals that voters are attentive to changes in parties' platforms, settling an ongoing debate in the literature, but that parties' ability to alter their policy image is inhibited by their participation in cabinet, adding to our understanding of how governance and co-governance influence party brands. In sum, voters seem to *fully* incorporate manifesto changes made by opposition parties, but only partially incorporate such changes made by cabinet parties. We argue that the difference is driven by cabinet parties' record of policy outputs, which crowds out campaign promises.

Our theoretical framework also yields new predictions regarding the uncertainty with which voters perceive the policy stands of parties. We find suggestive evidence that cabinet parties' positions are perceived more clearly than the opposition, strong evidence that clearer policy pronouncements reduce uncertainty in voters' perceptions, and stronger still evidence that uncertainty is greater before European Parliament (EP) elections relative to national elections (presumably due to an expressed lack of interest in EP elections).

We spend the lion's share of Section 5 discussing several families of open questions for future research. These research questions span every (democratic) institutional context and while all *can* be studied with the CCS framework, data, and modeling strategy that we present, none *must* be. Let's get started.

2 Building a Theoretical Argument

We present a framework for building and scrutinizing theoretical arguments to assess their plausibility and ultimately derive empirical expectations for testing. By doing so, we provide a path for researchers to deepen their understanding of the proposed causal process – the mapping of $x \rightarrow y$ – and generate expectations for how the event of interest influences voters' perceptions. This path formalizes basic assumptions about what perceptions are and how perceptions are updated, and pairs them with a rigorous process for assessing whether and how political events shape perceptions. Using this approach, researchers can organize past research, (re)situate their argument within that context, refine their theoretical argument, and potentially identify new or previously overlooked empirical implications. Importantly, this framework is not designed to burden researchers with a cumbersome checklist of criteria to meet, but rather to clarify and enhance arguments while refining expectations. We demonstrate its value by illustrating how the framework produces testable propositions regarding the effects of coalition membership and the publication of election manifestos on voters' perceptions.

Before we build the framework it is important to make clear the value we are studying, reiterating a passage from Section 1. Coarsening to a single point in a single jurisdiction, we can think of every party as having (at least) three policy positions. The first is its "true" position, or its actual, sincere policy intentions. The second is its strategically selected, advertised position, or, what the party *wishes voters to believe* its policy intentions are for the purpose of maximizing votes. The third is the voters' perception of the party position, which is what ultimately drives voters' behavior and therefore electoral returns. This Element is focused on perceptions and, as such, while parties' "true" positions or strategically selected positions may influence perceptions and should certainly be correlated with perceptions, they are inherently different theoretical concepts, worthy of study in their own right, but not the focus here.

2.1 Foundations

We assume that people use a spatial metaphor to organize information about the policy preferences of political actors such as candidates, parties, interest groups, themselves, and their peers. For simplicity, this organizing spatial structure is assumed to be unidimensional, where preferences across all policy jurisdictions can be collapsed to a position on that continuum. For example, increasing taxation to fund more government services might be described as "left," while reducing government services to lower taxation might be described as "right." Importantly, we need not assume that a party's position on one issue lies at the same point on the continuum as its position on any other issue, that positions are positively correlated across issues, or even that each party *has* a position on all issues. Additionally, we need not assume that the spatial orientation of any given policy – that is, more government services being "left" and fewer government services being "right" – is consistent across countries. The only organizing assumptions we need to make are that, generally, within a context or a given country at a specific time, political elites who generate and communicate information about parties' policy objectives tend to agree on the orientation of significant policy jurisdictions in the left–right space. This, in turn, constrains the typical voter's understanding of the orientation of significant policy jurisdictions in the left–right space.

Our theoretical framework builds on canonical models of opinion formation, for example Fiorina's (1981) model of partisan affiliations as a "running tally" of assessments, Bartels's (2002) Bayesian model of political assessments, and especially Zaller's (1992) "receive-accept-sample" (RAS) model of probabilistic response. Following each, we allow voters to encounter and accumulate (or not) new information regarding the policy positions of various parties. Like Zaller, we treat voter perceptions as distributions rather than points or stable "facts."

To refresh, the RAS model posits that we should understand political opinions, such as perceptions of party positions, as probabilistic realizations from a distribution rather than as fixed points. Zaller argued that the likelihood of a left response to some political stimulus is given by $L/(L+R)$, – that is, the number of left considerations over the total number of left and right considerations at the time the response is solicited.[9] In Zaller's model, voters *receive* considerations $y \in \{L, R\}$, *accept* them if they are conducive to their worldview, and *sample* from their distribution when asked their political opinion.

For our purposes, we relax the assumption that political views are binary, $y \in \{L, R\}$, and allow them to instead be continuous, $y \in (L, R)$ – where L and R are now the leftmost and rightmost policy positions; arbitrary bounds on $\mathbb{R}$ – and assume an individual's perception of a party is a random variable, defined by the distribution of messages on hand connoting its policy position, which is distributed $Y \sim N(\mu, \sigma^2)$. As such, we do not observe the random variable Y, but its realizations y.

A useful analogy for Y is to think of it as all the information a person possesses signaling the policy preferences of a party. If some party l declares its intentions to pursue *increases* in income taxes and welfare spending, and some

---

[9] As Zaller wrote about the American case, he used "L" and "C" or "liberal" and "conservative" to describe preferences.

party r declares its intentions to pursue *decreases* in income taxes and welfare spending, the leftward policy intentions of party l and the rightward policy intentions of party r may shape Y_l and Y_r such that $\mu_l < \mu_r$. The result is that, in expectation, voters will perceive party l as *left* of party r. If some party m declares its intentions to pursue *decreases* in income taxes but *increases* in welfare spending, this mix of leftward and rightward policy intentions may shape Y_m such that $\mu_l < \mu_m < \mu_r$ and $\sigma_l^2 = \sigma_r^2 < \sigma_m^2$. The result is that, in expectation, voters will perceive party m as *right* of party l and *left* of party r, and voters' perceptions of party m will be more *variable* than those of parties l and r.

There are many advantageous properties of this framework. For instance, the random variable Y can be ported into a Bayesian learning model (e.g., Achen 1992) to learn about the potential flexibility or calcification of perceptions as new signals are incorporated with the prior distribution. Alternatively, we can estimate the likelihood of the distribution's parameters given the observed data $L(\mu, \sigma^2 \mid Y = y)$, which of course can be modeled with covariates.

2.2 CCS Framework

Accepting perceptions as probabilistic draws, we turn our attention to considering which messages are assimilated such that they (re)shape that distribution – that is, what makes μ more "left" or more "right," and what influences σ^2 to be smaller or larger? Assume we have identified a political event and the information it connotes about a party's policy preferences. Also, assume away for the moment factors that may influence the information connoted by the event – all individuals would interpret the event identically for all parties in all systems. Will the policy content of the information be incorporated into perceptions of the party's policy position? We propose answering this question by considering three criteria: the signal's cost, credibility, and salience (CCS). Is the information sufficiently low *cost* in terms of both its availability (will the voter be exposed) and its complexity (will the voter understand) that voters can be reasonably expected to encounter and comprehend it? Is the information *credible* such that voters will find it indicative of real policy intent? And is the information sufficiently *salient* to voters that they will find it a relevant addition to their store of party preference signals?

Depending on the researcher's focus, CCS may be considered (nonexclusively) at the individual, party, or system level. In each case, CCS evaluation should be guided by the researcher's qualitative understanding of the event, individuals, parties, and systems; relevant extant research; and, of course, any new or existing evidence the researcher can bring to bear. If the researcher concludes that the signal's policy content is accessible, reliable, and meaningful, then the researcher may expect it to reshape voters' party perceptions. Note, however, that this is not a one-size-fits-all process. The CCS consideration may reveal that the cost of some information varies over characteristics of voters, or that the salience of some information may vary over characteristics of parties, etc. These revelations should in turn be utilized to refine empirical predictions.

These considerations are not new to this literature – for example, Falcó-Gimeno and Fernandez-Vazquez (2020) discuss at length the conditions under which voters will incorporate new information on parties – but formalizing a CCS framework is instructive and helps us contextualize differences in empirical consistency within the literature. For example, every article that has investigated the effect of multiparty government participation has found that entering into a coalition has a directionally consistent and statistically significant influence on how parties are perceived as a result of their co-governance (e.g. Fortunato and Stevenson 2013a; Plescia 2022; Hjermitslev 2023). We believe that this empirical consistency is due to the cost, credibility, and salience of cabinet formation. That is, government formation is perhaps the most widely reported political event in parliamentary democracies, making it one of the most, if not the most, available pieces of dynamic political information (Fortunato and Stevenson 2013b). The event conveys highly credible information on parties' ideological compatibility since the formation of a coalition cabinet is a public declaration of shared goals and values, as well as a public commitment to ongoing policy compromise. Finally, there is likely no event as salient to governance or the generation of policy outcomes as government formation. As such, it is little wonder that the relationship between voters' perceptions of parties and the parties' co-governance status is stable across many disparate studies.

2.2.1 Analytical Schema

This basic schema for assessing the cost, credibility, and salience of information relevant to parties' positions can be used to understand and reorganize nearly all previous contributions to this literature. For example, Adams, Weschle, and Wlezien (2021) argue that proximity to national elections decreases the *cost* of information about parties, which reshapes voters' perceptions of those parties. Fernandez-Vazquez and Somer-Topcu (2019) argue that leadership changes drive voters to perceive platform changes as more *credible*. Adams et al. (2006) argue that changes in party programs are more *salient* to niche party supporters and are therefore more impactful. Each event (or its policy information) has an associated level of cost, credibility, and salience – all of which may potentially vary at the individual, party, or system level – that should determine whether it influences voters' beliefs about that party's preferences.

While it seems intuitive and noncontroversial that researchers should assess these features of various events or information potentially connoting party preferences – and many researchers do – such practice is nonetheless far from ubiquitous. We believe it should be, and that adoption of this process will generate several beneficial returns. First, this discussion forces a degree of formalization of both the theoretical and empirical assumptions made by the researcher, most importantly: *Who* knows *what*, and *how* do they know it? If a researcher argues that a particular event will have a specific impact on how voters perceive parties, discussing the accessibility of the event should prompt the researcher to consider how voters will learn of it. Will voters observe the event directly, learn about it through media coverage, or otherwise absorb the relevant information (see, e.g., Fortunato 2021)?

Formalizing informational assumptions can help the researcher refine their expectations and potentially their empirical tests as well. For example, the formation of a coalition government is simple, nominal, and uncontroversial information: sufficiently simple and uncontroversial that it makes little difference whether voters watch the announcement of the cabinet formation live and hear it from the mouths of party leaders themselves, read about it in the newspaper, or hear about it from a coworker the next day – the cabinet is what it is. On the other hand, forecasts about the potential real-world effects of a policy proposal can be complex, cardinal, and controversial information: sufficiently complex and controversial that it may matter a great deal whether one learns about it from a budget office assessment, reads about it in the newspaper, or hears about it from a coworker. The opportunity for "slippage" in the information is greater, and contending with this slippage may push the researcher toward more nuanced empirical tests. Banducci, Giebler, and Kritzinger (2017) and Fernandez-Vazquez and Somer-Topcu (2019) take seriously potential differences in information accessibility to the great benefit of their research.

Second, the discussion can help clarify the processes through which events convey policy information, particularly when discussing the credibility of the signal. Fernandez-Vazquez (2018, 2019) argues that unpopular policy objectives are likely to be viewed as more credible by voters precisely because they are unpopular. In a framework where voters must distinguish between pandering and true intention, they are more likely to conclude that almost certainly damaging policy pronouncements must not be cheap talk.

A particularly insightful example comes from O'Brien (2019), who argues that parties will be perceived as more moderate after appointing women leaders. The argument is not rooted in any known empirical relationship between women party leaders and party policy moderation – indeed, O'Brien shows that parties with women leaders are slightly more extreme on average than those led by men. Rather, O'Brien argues that what makes the event's moderating signal credible is the pervasiveness and durability of certain gender stereotypes. These stereotypes lead voters *to infer* policy moderation from the selection of a woman leader, even if no moderation has occurred. That is, the event does not convey "real" policy information; instead, it triggers a reliable gender stereotype that is incorporated *as if* it were real policy information.

Third, the discussion presents an opportunity to clarify important qualitative differences between parties and their goals, histories, strategies, supporters, and more. One interesting example of this type of discussion is provided by Falcó-Gimeno and Fernandez-Vazquez (2020), who argue that the formation of coalition cabinets by unlikely or unexpected party constellations sends more salient policy signals to voters because these events are likely discordant with their priors. More recently, Meyer and Wagner (2019) and Wagner and Meyer (2023) have made issue salience a key part of parties' electoral strategies, arguing that parties need not actually change their policy commitments to reshape how voters perceive them in the policy space. Instead, the authors argue that parties may emphasize issues on which their *existing* positions are more or less left or right in order to shift voters' perceptions of their overall position, without appearing to "flip-flop" or renege on their previous stands. In other words, they provide evidence that parties behave according to our framework, consciously attempting to change the weights borne by certain pieces of information in voters' perceptual distributions.

It is also possible that certain events or types of information may simply be irrelevant for some parties. As we discuss later, parties in government and parties in opposition operate under different signaling constraints. While opposition parties are free to issue any statement they like, assuming the same level of credibility and salience, cabinet parties are constrained by their record of governance. Parties in government make policy, and the policies they produce are tangible and may be more salient to voters than potentially discordant policy statements. These dynamics were elegantly discussed by Bawn and Somer-Topcu (2012) when crafting their argument about how governing changes campaign strategies and were also detailed by Fortunato (2019b, 2021), who argued that coalition compromises can crowd out policy statements, making voters uncertain about what cabinet parties truly want.

Of course, clarifying these assumptions and discussing their plausibility also provide the reader with an opportunity for consideration and scrutiny, which should incentivize the researcher toward empirical justification if at all possible. Many of the questions raised here are, at heart, empirical questions for which the researcher may marshal evidence to support their key assumptions. Fortunato and Stevenson (2013a), for example, provide detailed information on how capable voters are of identifying parties in government when discussing the utility of using a coalition participation heuristic for drawing inferences about parties' preferences.

Given the postulation of a theoretically and substantively interesting relationship influencing voters' perceptions of a party's position – a partisan action or event, the policy information it connotes, and the manner in which this information will (re)shape voters' perceptions – the researcher's task, then, is to think through the probability of voters' exposure to this action or event and the likelihood that they view the policy information it connotes as credible and salient. We suggest the following process:

1. Identify partisan *event* and its *policy information* at the individual, party, or system level.
2. Assess the *cost* of the information.
3. Assess the *credibility* of the information.
4. Assess the *salience* of the information.
5. Identify potential *CCS moderators* at the individual, party, or system level.
6. Derive falsifiable *expectations* for the effect of the event on perceptions.

2.3 Application

Here, we walk through this process for two events – participation in multiparty government and the issuance of party platforms – focusing on the *party* level, as we will throughout this Element. This exercise necessarily ignores other interesting characteristics of individual voters (e.g., political interest, Adams, De Vries, and Leiter 2012), parties (e.g., leadership changes, Somer-Topcu 2017), and systems (e.g., number of parties, Carroll and Kubo 2018). Nonetheless, the number of substantively interesting hypotheses that this process yields, even when considering just these two central events, should demonstrate the potential utility of this approach for future research.

As mentioned, government formation is perhaps the least costly, most credible, and most salient piece of political information. This event receives a large amount of media coverage, increasing the probability that voters are exposed to the information. For example, Fortunato and Stevenson (2013a) show that between 75% and 97% of Dutch voters, depending on their political interest, can properly identify *at least* 11 of 13 political parties as being in the cabinet or opposition. The policy information associated with government formation should be considered both credible and salient by any reasonable metric. The cabinet holds a de jure monopoly on the legislative agenda, granting it exclusive control over changes to the status quo (Cox 1987). Empirically, cabinet participation is the single best predictor of whether a party can convert its policy promises into policy outcomes (Thomson et al. 2017), making cabinet participation the single greatest indicator of positive policy influence. In other words, there is a strong empirical case that voters observe the event – most voters know who governs with whom – and a compelling case to be made that the associated policy information should be perceived as credible and salient because the event bears more substantive policy consequences than any other event, save perhaps the electoral outcome that precedes it.

The policy information most likely communicated by participation in a coalition cabinet is that the member parties are ideologically compatible. We note that different studies have focused on different aspects of multiparty governance, but all derive the same policy signal. For example, Hjermitslev (2022, 2023) and Plescia (2022) focus on coalition *formation*, Fortunato (2019a, 2019b) and Klüver and Spoon (2020) focus on coalition *policymaking*, while Fortunato and Stevenson (2013a) and Adams, Ezrow, and Wlezien (2016) take a holistic approach – all conclude that the brand-updating policy information voters are likely to derive from coalition participation is that the partners are more ideologically similar than previously perceived. Fortunato (2021) discusses in great detail the rationale and evidence for this expectation, which we summarize here: (1) Coalition formation is a public declaration of an intent to cooperate and compromise, usually memorialized with an accounting of compromised policy objectives (the coalition agreement). (2) Institutional structures and party strategies conspire to ensure that the average policy outcome reflects some aggregation of all member parties' policy preferences. (3) Institutional constraints prevent member parties from publicly decrying policy proposals and outcomes during the government's tenure (collective responsibility).

Taken together, these factors should send a consistent signal regarding the policy stances of member parties. Referring back to the perceptions model shorthand, we should expect voters to update their perceptions of cabinet parties' positions (μ) as more ideologically similar to one another – to perceive member Party A as nudged in the direction of member Party B and vice versa. Summarizing our example of the process just enumerated, we expect that this policy information is received by voters, seen as credible and salient, and incorporated into their perceptions. Of course, the extant literature has found just this, and it is perhaps the strongest empirical relationship in this subfield.

What has not yet been directly addressed is the effect of cabinet formation on nonparticipants. Just as agreeing to co-governance sends a strong signal of policy compatibility, *not* supporting a government is a strong signal of policy incompatibility – that the nonparticipant has less in common with the cabinet than cabinet members do with one another. When coalition partners publicly consent to cooperation and compromise in forming their cabinet, opposing parties present themselves as the alternative to the incumbents and (explicitly or implicitly) declare their intention to derail the cabinet. Where institutional structures and party strategies conspire to ensure that policy outcomes represent aggregations of coalition members' preferences, those same structures are typically leveraged to exclude opposition input. And, while institutional constraints prevent cabinet parties from publicly decrying their partners' policy proposals, opposition parties typically criticize those proposals, endeavor to obstruct them, and ultimately vote against them on the floor of parliament. The same processes that should drive voters to perceive coalition parties as more similar to one another should also drive voters to perceive opposition parties as more *dis*similar from the cabinet, and we should expect that this signal is likely to be received by voters and considered credible and salient for the reasons discussed previously. We therefore predict that voters will update their perceptions of opposition party positions (μ) away from the governing coalition. In sum, one event – cabinet formation – is sending two types of policy information to voters: one for participants and one for nonparticipants. We can summarize with aforementioned the list:

1. *Event and policy information*: formation of coalition cabinet; coalition members are compatible with one another, members of the opposition are incompatible with the cabinet
2. *Cost*: low
3. *Credibility*: high
4. *Salience*: high
5. *Moderators*: none
6. *Expectations*: (a) Voters will perceive coalition partners as more similar to one another. (b) Voters will perceive opposition parties as more dissimilar from the cabinet.

The next event we consider is an electoral manifesto. The general – and, we believe, perfectly intuitive and sensible – expectation is that voters' perceptions of party brands should positively respond to the policy objectives outlined in the party's campaign platform. As noted in Section 2, despite the common sense nature of this expectation, research on it has produced surprisingly mixed results, ranging from an emphatic "yes" (Seeberg, Slothuus, and Stubager 2017), to "yes," but with effects that are small (Fernandez-Vazquez 2014) or delayed (Adams and Somer-Topcu 2009), to an emphatic "no" (Adams, Ezrow, and Somer-Topcu 2011). How can this be? Our contention, and a central motivation for this Element, is that the discord arises from a confluence of three factors: differences in data and measurement, modeling strategy and interpretation, and theoretical approach, which is the focus here.

How costly are manifestos to observe, and is their content credible and salient? We contend that manifestos are extraordinarily costly to observe; we do not believe it is at all likely that voters will read the electoral manifestos of the parties competing to represent them. These documents tend to be sufficiently long and unpleasant to read that even in quite small party systems, it is simply unreasonable to expect that many (or any) voters will consume the content directly.[10]

That said, we do contend that the information connoted by the event *is* low cost and accessible and therefore likely to be received by voters. This is because manifesto content – the policy objectives of parties competing for office – is typically the most salient aspect of electoral competition. Though voters might not read the manifesto itself, its content will be communicated by the media, issuing party, and perhaps even the party's opponents (though not necessarily accurately; see Somer-Topcu and Tavits 2023). Indeed, communicating the core policy objectives of the contestants, and allowing the contestants to scrutinize and debate the finer points of those objectives so that voters may understand the objectives and their potential virtues, is, to us, the *purpose* of the campaign. Moreover, campaigns are not only the core of party competition and the democratic process but also the period of time during which voters tend to be most attuned to political discourse. It is no wonder that recent research suggests that voters do, in fact, receive these policy objective messages throughout the campaign (Somer-Topcu, Tavits, and Baumann 2020).

The information in manifestos is credible for two central reasons. First, they are authored and issued directly by the parties themselves. Often, the document is composed, scrutinized, and formally voted upon by the party membership through a prescribed process (Scarrow, Webb, and Poguntke 2017), giving it a level of internal legitimacy that should translate to external credibility. Second, and more importantly, the pursuit of the manifesto's policy objectives *is* the party's raison d'être – parties are organized as policy-seeking institutions that compete for and retain office based on their policy objectives and outputs

---

[10] The 2010 UK Liberal Democrats' manifesto was a "brisk" 57 pages, compared to the 131-page document issued by their eventual cabinet partners, the Conservatives, that year.

(Aldrich 1995). This is evident in parties' empirical records of keeping their promises or delivering on the policy objectives declared in their manifestos, particularly if they enter government (Erikson, MacKuen, and Stimson 2002; Thomson et al. 2017). In other words, today's promises are credible because yesterday's promises were likely kept.

Finally, manifesto content should be among the most salient pieces of policy information that voters encounter. As noted, parties' policy commitments are typically the most important aspect of electoral competition and the manifesto is the official declaration of those commitments. In a sense, the manifesto *is* the party. Given the low cost of manifesto content and the high credibility and salience of these platforms we expect that they should be incorporated into voters' perceptions and drive a positive shift in the mean (μ) of voters' perception distributions (e.g., a leftward change in manifesto position should result in a leftward change in voters' perceptions).

Though we expect a strong, positive correlation between changes in parties' platforms and voters' perceptions, the manner in which platforms lead to perception changes should not be consistent across parties. We expect a party's *cabinet participation* to weight the salience of the manifesto in reshaping voters' perceptions such that manifestos carry greater weight in voters' perceptions of opposition parties than cabinet parties. This is similar to what Bawn and Somer-Topcu (2012) have argued. Continuing our thread, parties in government spend the legislative term assembling a record of observable policymaking processes and outcomes, whereas parties in opposition do not. Hence, in the lead-up to the election, the policy *commitments* of opposition parties should be the most relevant consideration when voters update their perceptions of these parties' positions, while cabinet parties might see their statements "crowded out" by their record of governance. The policy information communicated by manifestos might be equally costly and credible for cabinet and opposition parties, but substantially less salient for cabinet parties than for their counterparts in opposition. We therefore expect that voters will be responsive to changes in party platforms, but that these responses will be much stronger for opposition parties than for governing parties.

1. *Event and policy information*: issuance of electoral manifesto; its policy commitments
2. *Cost*: low (though not directly observed)
3. *Credibility*: high
4. *Salience*: generally high
5. *Moderators*: information is more salient for opposition parties than cabinet parties

6. *Expectations*: (a) Voters will update their perceptions of parties positively to manifesto content. (b) Response is more positive for opposition parties than cabinet parties.

To sum up our application of the CCS framework, and limiting our discussion to just the mean (μ) of voters' perceptions, we have derived four testable hypotheses (two of which are novel to the literature) by considering just two events and one characteristic of parties.[11] This discussion held individual-level differences across voters, such as gender, party affiliation, or political interest, constant. We also held constant alternative characteristics of parties, such as their family, gender mix, or internal rules, and characteristics of systems, such as development, electoral permissiveness, or federalism. Investigating how these factors might condition the cost, credibility, and salience of the policy information transmitted by political events is almost certain to reveal new avenues for investigation and improve our understanding of the construction, maintenance, and (in)stability of party brands.

We note that this exercise is not critical for each and every covariate in each and every empirical model. As research is produced, we accumulate findings and reach some consensus on how certain factors work in the perceptual process, making this exercise unnecessary for a growing number of covariates. However, we do view this process, or something akin to it, as fairly critical for theoretical discussion and the derivation of empirical implications. This exercise is not only valuable for elucidating arguments and enhancing transparency, but it can also refine proposed causal processes and, therefore, empirical expectations.

3 Data, Measurement of Perceptions, and Modeling Choices

Our dataset, Sophia: The Party Placements Data, is our attempt to build a large, inclusive, common pool of data on voters' perceptions of party positions, aggregating all parliamentary electoral surveys contained in all modules of three cooperative cross-national surveying projects: the European Voter Project (EVP 1956–1998), the European Election Studies (EES 1989–2019), and the Comparative Study of Electoral Systems (CSES 1996–2019). We also added several national election studies (ES) not included in EVP or CSES, in order to fill gaps left by the core series. The principal inclusion criterion was whether or not the survey asked respondents for spatial evaluations of relevant political

---

[11] We return to these events in a later section to consider their effects on the variance (σ^2) of voters' perceptions.

parties. The consolidated raw dataset consists of 321 surveys and 1,988 party-time observations, comprising more than 3 million respondent evaluations. Our analytical sample, after marrying it to other data sources needed for our final analysis, restricting to parliamentary systems, and calculating a lag, comprises 1329 party-time observations, which is about 10 times the average number of survey parties analyzed in the extant literature. This sample covers 389 parties across 32 European parliamentary democracies and spans 54 years (from 1965 to 2019).[12] The countries we analyze here are: Australia, Austria, Belgium, Canada, Croatia, Czech Republic, Denmark, Estonia, Finland, Germany, Greece, Hungary, Iceland, Ireland, Israel, Italy, Japan, Latvia, Lithuania, Luxembourg, Malta, the Netherlands, New Zealand, Norway, Poland, Portugal, Romania, Slovakia, Slovenia, Spain, Sweden, and the United Kingdom.[13]

The data are arranged so that each row corresponds to a specific respondent's placement of political parties on a left–right ideological scale within each country survey. This is assessed using standard survey questions such as, "In politics, people sometimes talk of left and right. Where would you place [party name] on a scale from 0 to 10, where 0 represents the left and 10 represents the right?" In addition to our principal covariate – that is, the respondent's left–right placement of the parties – we have also retained the respondent's gender, age, education, income, an indicator of whether they identify with any political party (and the party they are evaluating), retrospective evaluation of the country's economic situation, vote intention, previous vote, and their own left–right self-placement.

Given the variations in structures, scales, and response choices provided to respondents across different surveys, we have harmonized the responses in order to make them comparable across studies. The harmonization of the data is essential for valid cross-survey and cross-country comparisons, as well as for the empirical analyses conducted in Section 4. Details of the harmonization process alongside descriptions of each variable within our dataset are outlined in Appendix B of the Supplementary Material. In general, this process follows the guidance laid out by Duch and Stevenson (2008).

In the remainder of this section, we provide a brief discussion on the standard approach for measuring the dependent variable in the field, using *sample*

---

[12] Although the raw aggregated data include other democracies, we restrict our estimation sample to parliamentary systems to avoid the complexities inherent in presidential and semi-presidential systems, such as divided governments or cohabitation. Moreover, these systems exhibit significant variations in the institutional policy making powers (e.g., veto and decree powers) vested in the head of government (Silva 2023). These distinct configurations can create fundamentally different patterns of conflict and cooperation between parties.

[13] The list of countries and their observation frequencies can be found in Table B1 of the Supplementary Material (available online at www.cambridge.org/fortunato-et-al).

means, then describe our preferred data to measure, which we call Sophia. Following that, we highlight the variability found in model specifications and estimation practices within the literature. Lastly, we introduce a simple, flexible model specification that allows the researcher to recover all short- and long-term effects of their key covariates.

3.1 Measurement of Perceptions

3.1.1 Sample Means

The following discussion presumes that the estimand the researcher is wanting to recover is the change in voter perceptions of a party in response to an observable party characteristic or event, where the experimental analogue would be a within-respondent pre–post difference in perception given intervention relative to control. To our reading of the extant literature, this accurately describes the goal of nearly every study utilizing voter perceptions as the dependent variable. The points we make in what follows are appropriate to several other applications of the measurement, but they are targeted at this specific application.

Survey means are the industry standard dependent variable in this literature. Analysts simply average all respondent placements of the parties being evaluated and use this as the general measure of how voters perceive those parties' ideological positions. This is intuitive, efficient, transparent, and easily reproducible; four highly valued criteria in scientific research. However, we see this approach as having (at least) three considerable drawbacks specific to this application, some of which are special cases of the general problems in sample mean analyses discussed by Lewis and Linzer (2005).

The first potential problem with survey means is a high degree of variability in who places the parties. "Missing" responses appear in the data as a variety of categories, including "haven't heard of the left–right scale," "haven't heard of the party," "don't know where to place the party," and refused. That is, survey respondents will often choose not to offer an estimate of a party's ideological position for any number of reasons, but we suspect that a primary reason is a lack of familiarity with the party. Indeed, Ezrow, Tavits, and Homola (2014) find a very strong correlation between the proportion of respondents that place a party and its size. At the individual level, the tendency to guess in a response is strongly related to the respondent's political sophistication (proxied by education) and age (young are more likely to guess, Powell 1989, p. 209). This may induce selection bias, yielding systematically *better* placements for smaller parties, because primarily high interest respondents are offering placements for them. That ideologically extreme parties tend to be smaller suggests

Table 3 Frequency and percentage of different categories of missing values in the CSES (Modules 1-5)

	Frequency	Percentage
Not missing	720,284	79.5
No MARPOR code	114,879	12.7
Refused/no answer	8,754	1.0
Don't know	51,860	5.7
Haven't heard of that party	5,718	0.6
Haven't heard of left–right	4,267	0.5
Total	**905,762**	**100**

systematic correspondence between placement accuracy (and uncertainty) and parties' policy programs – that is, the most common independent variable in this literature.

Table 3 gives a snapshot of the missing values in Modules 1-5 of the CSES. Almost four-fifths (79.5%) of the responses are valid and 14% are missing for reasons due to unavailable or incorrect MARPOR codes (12.7%) or response refusal (1.0%). A smaller percentage of respondents provide a qualitative non-response, including "don't know" (5.7%), "haven't heard of the party" (0.6%), and "don't know/use the left–right scale" (0.5%). A sizeable percentage of the respondents therefore provides a nonresponse that may be correlated with their demographics or partisan beliefs.

We illustrate these patterns of missingness for respondents in Table 4, across some common respondent variables. Each row shows the proportion of missingness in party placements for the observed value of the indicated covariate – for example, respondents aged 18–30 years failed to place a party in 9.6% of their opportunities. For all but one of the variables in Table 4, there is a clear ordinal relationship between the covariate values and party placement missingness. The one exception, *age*, has a curvilinear relationship where missingness is higher for the youngest (18–30) and oldest (65+) categories than in the intermediate ranges. The other cells show that missingness decreases with education and income, is higher among females than males, and is lower among those who express a partisan identification or previously voted for that party. By far the starkest difference is between those who provided a left–right self placement (5.0%) and those who did not (66.7%), suggesting differences in overall familiarity with the spatial metaphor for organizing political actors. Most respondents "get it," but some categorically do not.

Table 4 Average percentage of missingness across relevant groups

	Miss %
Age	
18/30	9.6
31/40	8.6
41/50	8.2
51/64	8.2
65/max	10.0
Education	
<High school	14.5
High school	8.7
>High school	4.0
Income	
Lower 25th	12.0
Middle 50th	6.2
Upper 25th	4.8
Gender	
Female	11.0
Male	6.7
Partisan identification	
In-partisan	3.1
Out-partisan	8.9
Nonpartisan	6.3
Vote choice$_{t-1}$	
Yes	4.5
No	8.8
Self-placement	
Yes	5.0
No	66.7

As another illustration, consider the British 1997 elections with three parties' placements available in the CSES: Conservatives, Labour, and Liberal Democrats. If our suspicions about missingness are correct, we would expect to see higher rates of respondents failing to place the smaller of the three parties (Liberal Democrats), but more certainty surrounding those placements than the larger parties. Indeed, the percentage of respondents who do not place the Liberal Democrats (23.6%) is higher than either Conservatives (19.8%) or Labour (17.8%), but the standard error of those placements is higher for Conservatives (2.7) and Labour (2.4) relative to the Liberal Democrats (1.6). The descriptives suggest that this is a function of the Liberal Democrats' placements being primarily offered by those who are wealthier, more educated, and partisan. Further, if we constrain the large-party responses to only the subset that placed the Liberal Democrats, the standard errors of the large-party placements shrink by about 5%. This suggests that average placement of bigger parties – such as Conservatives and Labour – incorporate a wider swath of possibly lower information respondents than smaller parties.

Overall, this basic analysis would suggest that party placements are vulnerable to bias related to nonresponse. While there is a risk of systematic bias due to these correlations, a multiple imputation model (described in later) that incorporates those variables offers promising estimates of those missing placements.

A second potential problem with survey means is that they are aggregating the placements of very different kinds of respondents in a uniform manner. For example, we are aggregating the placements of the young, who may have only recently begun paying attention to politics and formulating their perceptions of these parties' positions, with the old, who may have formed their perceptions decades ago and not updated them since. We are also aggregating the perceptions of party supporters, who presumably have a much better idea of what that party stands for, with non-supporters. The distribution of respondent types being aggregated is critical because these distributions are likely to vary across *surveys* as the sample of respondents varies, and, across *parties* as the relationship between respondents and parties varies. That is, some parties have more supporters, and therefore a higher proportion of high quality placements, than others; some parties (likely newer parties) are more familiar to younger respondents than older respondents. These differences can induce bias that is systematically correlated to key covariates in ways that are both known and unknown.

A third potential problem with survey means is that they require strong assumptions for comparability. If we compare the mean placement of UK Labour in 2010 to its mean placement in 2015, we assume that the sample of respondents in 2010 is, if not identical, sufficiently representative of the sample of respondents in 2015 to ignore the possibility of differences in placements as a function of the sample demographics. At first blush, this is not an unreasonable assumption – electoral surveys are specifically designed to be representative and survey administrators take great pains to calculate respondent weights to achieve representativeness. However, in practice, these weights are nearly always ignored. In our meta-analysis, we failed to uncover a single example of scholars noting that they used sample weights in their estimation (of course, this does not preclude the possibility that they used the weights in the analysis without mentioning it). And, importantly, the weights are calibrated to the *sample entrants*, not the *vector-responding* participants. This means that, even if the weights are utilized by the researcher, failing to impute for missingness or otherwise account for nonresponse would disrupt the weighted quantity of interest. There is also the simpler, but more dramatic problem that different electoral studies are trying to capture fundamentally different electorates. Sweden's Riksdag electorate is a *different population* than Sweden's EP electorate, and surveys administered in advance of these elections are calibrated accordingly.

To summarize, sample means of left–right placements are intuitive, efficient, transparent, and easily reproducible, but nonetheless subject to biases induced by non-ignorable patterns of missingness, covariances in party-respondent characteristics, and incredible sampling assumptions. The result is that using sample means leaves scholars vulnerable to both known and unknown inferential threats that may induce systematic biases in ways that vary across demographic groups and party types.

3.1.2 Measurement Strategy

We tackle nonresponse first, which systematically varies with individual- and party-level characteristics. Multiple imputation allows us to use our knowledge of the origins of missing party placements and the wealth of covariates available in the Sophia data to predict, with appropriate degrees of uncertainty, missing values of left–right party placement (King et al. 2001; Honaker et al. 2011).

As noted, previous research has identified various individual-level characteristics that make respondents more or less likely to be able to place themselves and parties on a left–right scale (Bartels 1986; Powell 1989; Alvarez and Franklin 1994). This existing research can guide our choices on which covariates are critical to include in the imputation model and suggests that the model requires information related to gender, age, education, income, left–right self-placement, previous vote choice, vote intention, and whether or not the respondent identifies with the party they are evaluating. The imputation model, from which we derive 5 imputed data frames, allows unit-time trends according to party and year and we set logical bounds on imputed values, treating demographic responses (education, female, income, partisan) as ordinal, vote choices as nominal, and allowing continuous imputation of age, party placements and self-placements, but constraining those imputations to the interval observed in the raw data – age $\in [16, 119]$ and left–right placements $\in [0, 10]$.[14]

3.1.3 Aggregation Problems in Left–Right Placements

The second and third concerns we discussed regarding survey means pertain to aggregating the perceptions of different types of individuals, in different proportions, for different parties – this obviously perturbs our ability to recover our target estimand, as some party perceptions will be significantly higher or lower accuracy and certainty than others. We first discussed problems related to survey respondent–party relationships that may lead to systematic differences in the mean and variance of party placements. For example, different parties may have quite large or quite small numbers of supporters, changing the mix of high- and low-affinity (or expertise) placements for parties according to their popularity. Alternatively, some parties may have quite extreme party memberships and quite extreme voters have been shown to have systematically different perceptions of party locations (Fortunato and Stevenson 2013b; Fortunato, Stevenson, and Vonnahme 2016). We then discussed problems induced by temporal variability in aggregate sample characteristics. Comparing survey means for a particular party across surveys imposes strict (but almost never discussed) assumptions regarding the similarity of samples across instruments – assumptions that are unlikely to hold in most instances and de jure violated in instances in which the electorate being sampled differs (as is the case when comparing across national and European electoral surveys). It is tempting to think that these sampling differences will just be normally distributed noise, but they are not – they capture population trends in addition to sampling variability. For example, while Italy's population has aged rapidly in the postwar period, Germany's population has aged much more slowly, and, in fact, the country grew younger between 2015 and 2020.

To avoid these issues, our approach is to estimate a distribution of party placements for a *particular respondent*. By holding constant the characteristics

---

[14] Eliminating the bounds makes imputation more efficient, but makes subsequent description and modeling of the data messy (particularly limited-variable models popular for modeling typically discrete survey response).

of respondents (within and across party survey), the potential biases induced from covariate imbalance within or across sampling units are ameliorated. That is, the same properties that make controlled comparison across units in a linear regression model an unbiased and efficient estimator of a particular correlation also facilitate efficient predicted values that allow for more efficient cross-unit comparison of, in this case, voters' perceptions of party brands.

This approach – generating perceptions for a particular respondent to use as the dependent variable in estimation – is analogous to using a survey mean where all characteristics of the sample (its average age, proportion of party supporters, etc.) are interacted with all regressors to account for potential sample differences across observations (survey parties), and then interpreting effects for a particular sample portfolio (e.g., the sample we observe for Danish Venstre in 2011). Our approach, however, redistributes effort from estimation and interpretation to preliminary measurement of the dependent variable. This makes estimation more efficient (as there is no need to interact regressors with sample characteristics) and interpretation simpler.

The particular respondent we have chosen is the global mode of our full sample – the package of values that collectively occurs most frequently in our data. This is a 40-year-old woman with a secondary education, median self-placement, and middle-class income who does not identify with the party she is evaluating. We call these values "Sophia," which is both the most common name in Europe at present and the Greek word for wisdom, which we find appropriate given that this is a type of wisdom-of-crowds approach to capturing party brand perceptions. The intuition behind this approach is similar to Lax and Phillips's (2009) post-stratification approach. However, where their focus is modeling *in* the correct distribution of population characteristics, our focus is modeling *out* all population characteristics, such that we may assess how party events have changed the manner in which the party is perceived by a common individual, without potential bias induced by changing characteristics of a sample.

We derive the Sophia placements as follows.[15] For each party in each survey, we regress perceptions of that party on respondent age, education, gender, ideological self-placement, income, and an indicator for whether or not the

---

[15] A strength of this archetypal approach is that one can generate estimates for any particular configuration of covariates. Indeed, in Appendix C we reproduce our models based on estimates of Jack – low education, low income, younger, nonpartisan, male – and Jurgen – high education, high income, older, partisan, male. While the persistence rates vary in predictable ways given their demographic profile (i.e., Jurgen has a higher persistence rate than Jack), the theoretical results echo the findings presented in this Element with the weights attributed to manifesto positions and co-governance varying slightly.

respondent supports the party in question. We fit the data with a double-truncated normal regression model. This is similar to the typical normal-linear model, with the caveat that the probability density function is constrained to a finite interval, in this case $[0, 10]$, rather than $(-\infty, \infty)$ (Tobin 1958). This approach both provides more sensible predictions and frees us from assuming symmetry in error probability, which is only likely to hold for parties near the center. In other words, the density of placements (or the error distribution) for Germany's centrist Christian Democratic Union is likely quite symmetric in the limit, whereas the error distribution for Germany's Die Linke – the leftmost party in parliament for the past two decades – is almost certain to be quite asymmetric, and truncating the probability density function allows this to manifest in estimation and prediction. We estimate this regression once for each survey party in all five of our imputed data frames. For each imputed frame, we take 200 samples from the information matrix, following Tomz, Wittenberg, and King (2001) to predict Sophia, resulting in 1,000 total vectors of our dependent variable, reflecting the uncertainty from both the imputations and the party survey regression estimates.

Let us first examine those error properties to show that they are sensible relative to those we can derive in relation to survey means. Figure 2 plots the standardized uncertainty estimates for Sophia and survey means against their left–right position. For Sophia, the uncertainty is the standard deviation of the distribution of estimates (those 1,000 draws for each observation); for survey means, the uncertainty is the standard deviation of the raw placements. Both are rescaled to have mean 0 and standard deviation of 1 across placements to help ease the comparison. Two striking patterns stand out immediately. First, the level of typical variation in uncertainty among the survey means is substantially larger than the variability in Sophia uncertainty, which is muted and driven primarily by a handful of outliers (those outlying parties are new, small entrants in primarily new democracies). In other words, the median absolute difference between all survey means' uncertainty estimates and the mean of that distribution is more than 150% larger than the median absolute difference between all Sophia uncertainty estimates and the mean of that distribution. The second pattern is that uncertainty in survey means is much more responsive to left-right position than the Sophia uncertainty estimates. Moderate parties have much larger uncertainty estimates than their extreme counterparts when using survey means. We believe this is a manifestation of the non-response bias we discussed earlier – smaller, more extreme parties are placed by more attentive respondents on average.

Though some parties may find it advantageous to take ambiguous positions and allow voters to see in them what they wish to see (Somer-Topcu 2015),

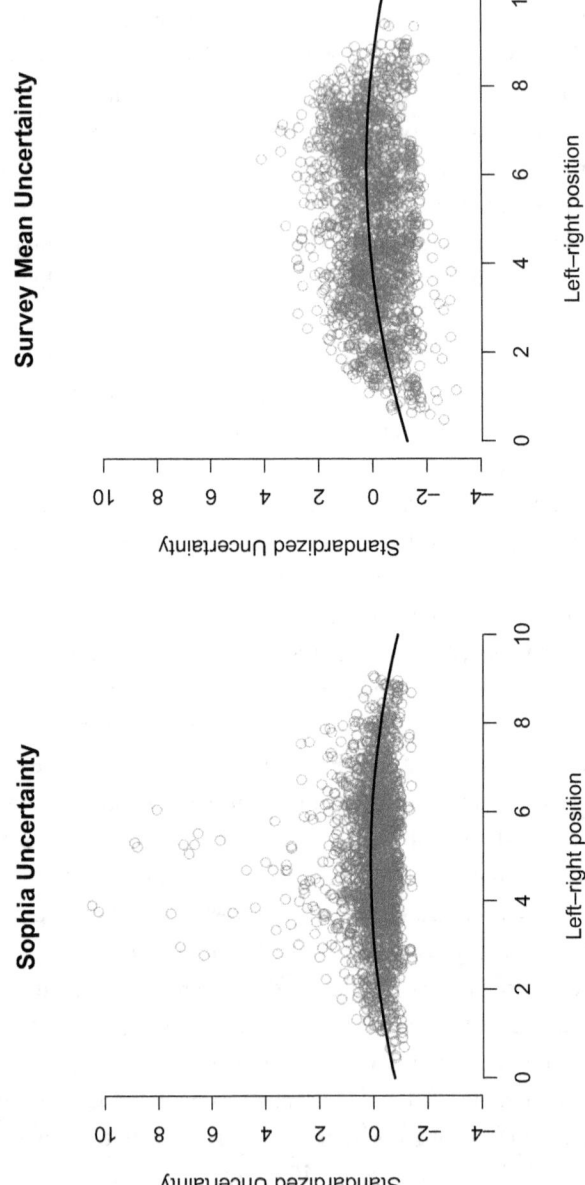

Figure 2 Comparing error properties of Sophia and survey means

most moderate parties in our data are well-known quantities who have been competing under a similar platform for decades. These are primarily Christian Democratic parties, Social Democratic parties, and moderate liberal parties, who tend to be older and somewhat more successful than their extreme counterparts. Indeed, if we were to plot parties' ages against their position extremity we would recover a negative relationship – older parties are more moderate on average. So why should perceptions of these parties be so much more uncertain? Our answer is that they should *not* be, and this reflects underlying issues utilizing raw survey means and standard deviations that are prone to a variety of biases due to unmodeled characteristics of parties and respondents that vary systematically according to other characteristics – for example, position – that researchers often care about. The nature of the response scale should induce some small parabolic relationship between extremity and error because placements of the most extreme parties can only be "wrong" in one direction, but we do not believe that this should be anywhere near as intense as it is for the survey means' uncertainty.

We now compare Sophia placements to the survey means in Figure 3, using filled gray triangles to indicate survey mean placements that fall within Sophia's 95% quantile band and hollow circles to indicate mean placements falling outside that band. The figures shows that the measures are highly correlated, as they should be, but still show systematic points of difference. Of course, there is general variance between the two estimates – most points fall off the 1:1 correlation lines. But the shape of that variance is not symmetric about 0, as survey means produce placements that are more extreme on average, relative to the Sophia placement. Essentially, survey means push parties on the left of the median more left and parties on the right of the median more right, relative to the (mean of the distribution of) Sophia estimates. Further, just about all of the extreme outlying placements – the parties whose survey mean deviates the most from their Sophia estimate – are outlying toward the extreme.

We can get a better sense of this by examining a subset of the data. The left pane of Figure 4 plots the (rank-ordered) estimates for the four largest parties (CDU, FDP, Greens, SPD) in Germany, one of the smaller party systems in our sample. Shaded points indicate the mean Sophia estimate, and the lines correspond to Sophia's 95% quantile band. Hollow black circles show the survey mean estimate for the same party. The figure shows that, in general, the survey mean estimate is left of the Sophia estimate for left parties and right of the Sophia estimate for right parties. Often, but certainly not always, the survey mean is outside of Sophia's 95% quantile band. Several factors contribute to this – the imputation process, bias induced by nonresponse for the means, and,

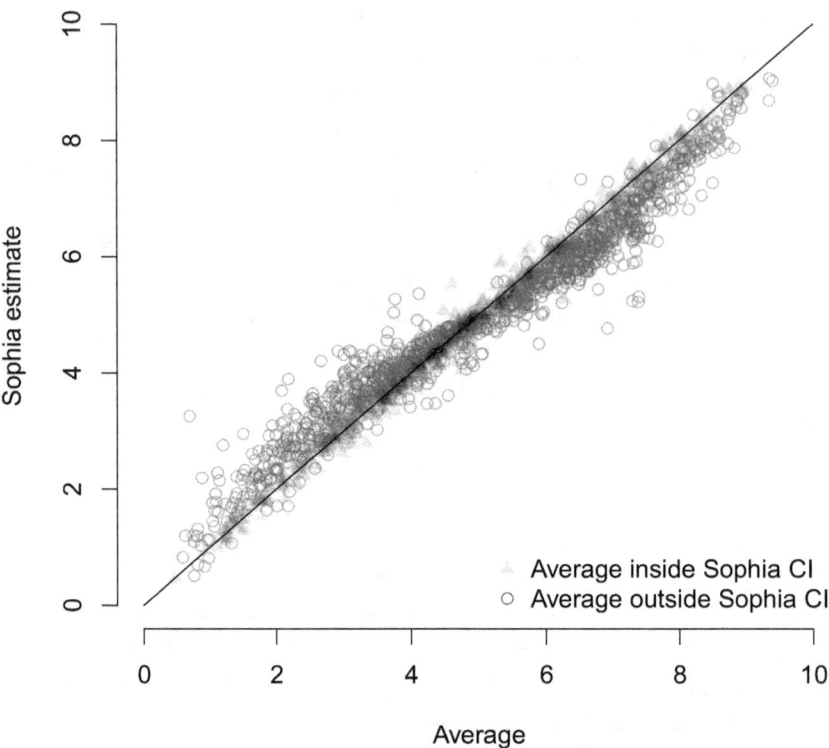

Figure 3 Comparing Sophia estimates to survey means.

of course, the fact that Sophia models the perceptions of a moderate, middle-income woman while survey means aggregate the placements of all those who offer a placement of that party. It is possible that Sophia just has more moderate, less polarized views of the political landscape than the typical survey respondent who offers a placement. This is not a problem for the analyst as our focus is nearly always on modeling voter responses to party events, rather than the "accuracy" of voter perceptions as a function of sample characteristics. Stability in the characteristics of the individual making the placement is important to recovering the typical response to party events.

Another way to compare the measures is to track their progress over time. The right pane of Figure 4 plots the Sophia estimates (solid lines) with 95% quantile band (bands) and survey mean placement (black dotted lines) for Germany's Christian and Social Democratic parties over the sample period. Overall variability is comparable, and the estimates often track together, but not always, and some directional shifts are even at odds from time to time.

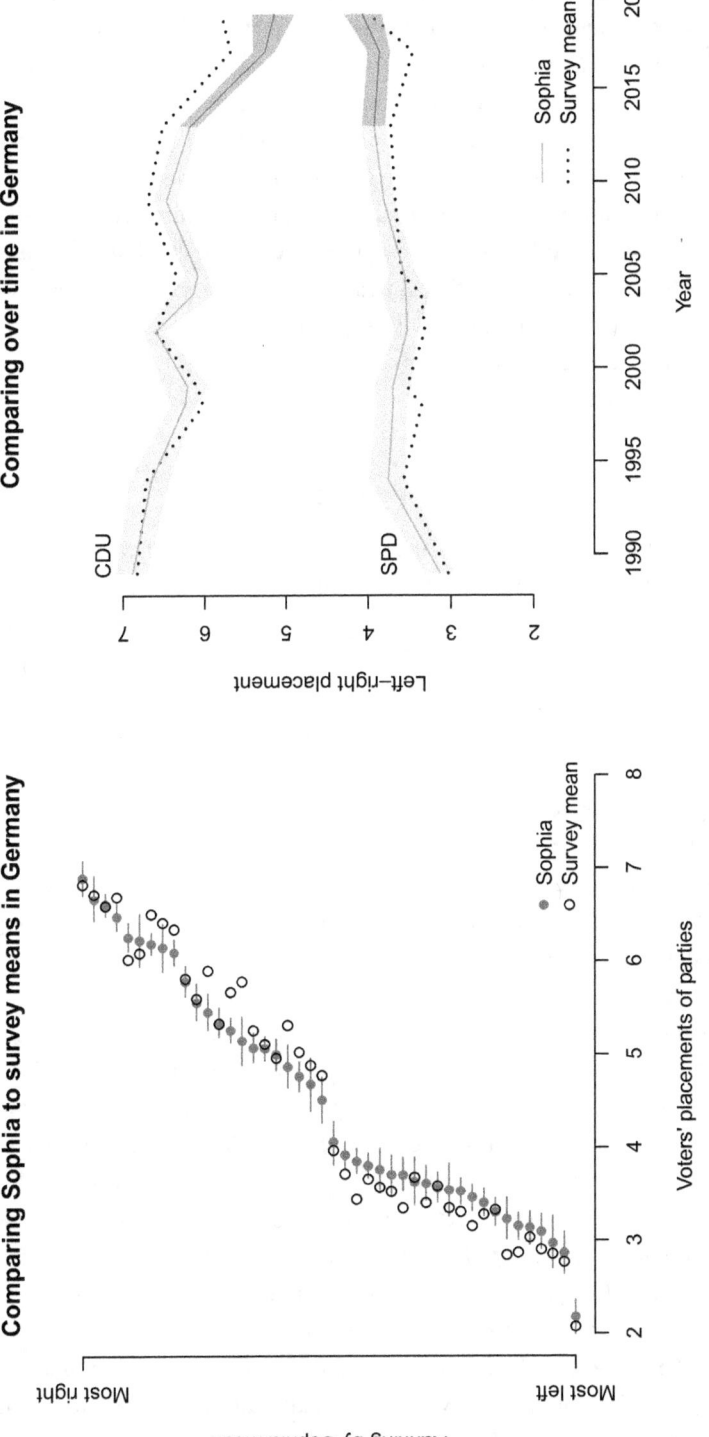

Figure 4 Comparing estimates for Germany.

This is particularly manifest in the case of the CDU and SPD following their coalescence in 2013 and continued co-governance through the end of the sample period, which we have highlighted in the figure. In keeping with theoretical expectations over the impact of coalition partnership, Sophia reflects the more or less monotonic convergence of voters' perceptions of CDU and SPD brands from 2013, but survey means do not. These perceptual changes are occurring during a period of manifesto stasis for both parties, making the divergent shifts between Sophia and survey means remarkable. Notice also that both estimates are relatively stable. We believe that this stability has been an underemphasized quality of voters' perceptions to date, potentially because survey means may have been obscuring it, particularly in small or noisy samples. Section 4 discusses this in more detail.

3.2 Modeling Choices

Our theoretical framework suggests that voters' perceptions should be fairly durable, but not unchangeable. In more concrete terms, we expect persistence estimates – the extent to which perceptions of a party yesterday predict perceptions of the party today, or, covariance in the distribution of relevant messages connoting party positions yesterday and today – should be high, but statistically and substantively less than 1. To clarify, a persistence estimate of 1 would mean that perceptions at $t - 1$ are 100% manifest at t, or, that perceptions are *unchangeable*. Conversely, a persistence estimate of 0 would mean that perceptions at $t - 1$ are completely unrelated to perceptions at t. We expect perceptions can be changed, but that change is limited and, for lack of a better term, difficult. Importantly, different types of events should have differing impacts on perceptions in the short and long term, and these differences are estimable.

This general expectation comports with extant theoretical research suggesting that parties have incentives to create stable brands (e.g., Aldrich 1995; Adams 2001; Cox and McCubbins 2005), and empirical research claiming that positions should generally be durable and fairly resilient to shocks in the long term. Dalton and McAllister (2015, p. 776) note that significant changes in perceptions across election cycles are rare events and conclude that "the predominant pattern is for party continuity over time." Voters' persistence in party perceptions is also noted in Fernandez-Vazquez (2014) and Fernandez-Vazquez and Somer-Topcu (2019). Adams, Bernardi, and Wlezien (2020, pp. 1163–1164) call this a "party reputation effect" and note that perceptions of parties' positions decay very gradually and are quite sticky; "in other words, there is a strong, if imperfect, memory to party positions..."

Given the general understanding that party brands are created and maintained (or changed) over time, nearly all research in this field is focused on how perceptions of these brands change over time – how does entering into a coalition cabinet or the issuance of a new electoral manifesto change how voters perceive a party's policy brand? However, approaches to the dynamic nature of the data-generating process as manifest in empirical models have been highly variable. Recalling our exploratory literature review table in Section 1, less than half of the surveyed articles included a lagged dependent variable. In this section, we first probe the general expectation that perceptions of brands are relatively stable. We then discuss building dynamic models of brands, illustrating how statistical specifications lock in theoretical assumptions, constraining certain relationships from manifesting and causing "spillover" into recovered relationships on correlated variables. Much of this work is simply clarifying some central theoretical claims from the time-series literature, but we also take care to show rather than tell how certain assumptions (and their violations) may influence model estimates.

3.2.1 Are Individuals' Perceptions Time-Stable?

The 2014–2022 British Election Study (BES) Internet Panel (Waves 1–23) provides an excellent data source to examine stability in party placements. Respondents in the BES can participate in multiple waves of surveys, which allows us to compare perceptions *within-respondent*. In other words, rather than hope that our model specification can control for potential confounders in cross-section surveys, BES panel data allow us to directly observe the stability of peoples' perceptions of party brands over time (about every four months on average). Given that we are comparing within-respondent, observed shifts in these placements can primarily be attributed to changing party- or system-level features (such as party strategy, cabinet formation, etc). More importantly, once we discover how stable individuals' perceptions of a particular party are, we can consider this level of stability something of a benchmark for our aggregate models later in the Element.

We begin by reformatting the data into a respondent-party structure across the 23 waves. Respondents are asked to place the Conservatives, Labour, Liberal Democrats, and UKIP (prior to wave 17) on a 0–10 left–right scale in all but a few waves (excepting 1, 13, 14, and 19). If we calculate the absolute change in placements from the previous measured wave at the individual-party level, we can get a sense of the average party brand stability within-individual. The mean absolute change is quite small (1.06) with a similarly small variance (1.5 standard deviation). About 90% of placements are within two units

Table 5 *Autoregressive Distributed Lag* (1;0) results of the individual persistence of perceptions in the British Election Study Internet Panel

	ADL (1;0)
Perceptions$_{t-1}$	0.84*
	(0.0006)
Constant	0.91*
	(0.004)
N	773,923
Adjusted R^2	0.70

of the previous placement. Indeed, 42.9% of the respondents provide the same placement in successive waves, and another 33.6% (or 12.9%) provide placements that are one (or two) units from the previous placement. This is a level of stability that may have shocked Zaller and Feldman (1992), who documented comparatively quite inconsistent political attitudes on core questions (of the time) regarding American respondents' preferences for government services or cooperating with Russia.

To present a more familiar and rigorous evaluation, we can estimate a simple time-series model in which we regress each respondent's perception of each party on their (one-wave) lagged perception. In time-series jargon, this is an *Autoregressive Distributed Lag* model (ADL) 1;0, where the first value, 1, indicates a lag on the dependent variable (one unit) and the second value, 0, indicates the lag on the independent variables (0, as in this case, there are no other covariates). In Table 5, the coefficient for the lagged dependent variable is highly efficient and close to (but statistically distinct from) 1. The coefficient is 0.84, which means that a 1-unit change in the prior placement translates into a 0.84-unit change in the current placement.[16] The R^2 is 0.70, suggesting that about 70% of the total wave-to-wave within-respondent variation in party placement can be explained by the prior placement. Taken together, the quite high persistence estimate, and large amount of total variation explained solely by the lagged DV, suggests that voters' perceptions of party brands should be fairly stable on average, though still malleable. This tells us that our

---

[16] We suspect that this persistence rate may be slightly elevated because it excludes those who attrite from the panel. Frankel and Hillygus (2014, p. 342) show that "those who attrite are more likely to be young, non-white, less educated and less connected to their communities." As we show in Appendix D, respondents with these characteristics typically have lower persistence rates so natural attrition is likely to increase the overall persistence rate.

Voters' Perceptions of Party Brands

Perceptions of UK parties 1982–2019

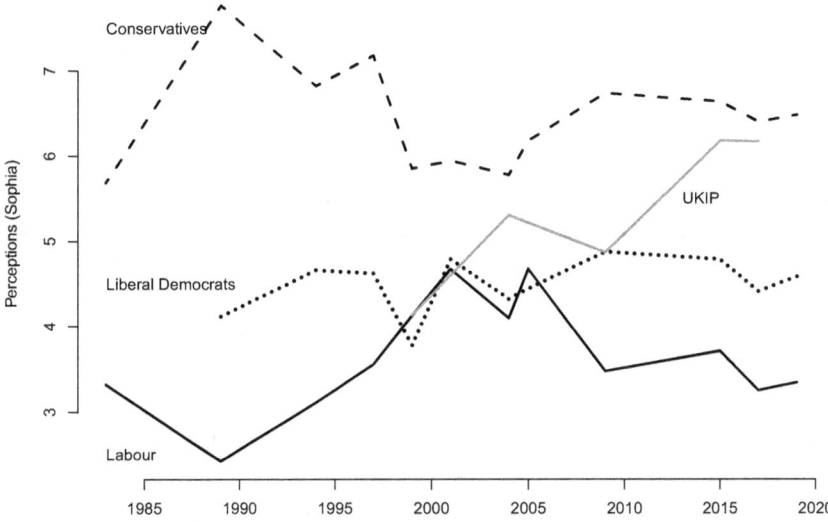

Figure 5 Sophia perceptions for British parties from 1983–2019

aggregate models, if they are well specified, should also recover high persistence estimates that approach – but are statistically differentiable – from 1 and that 0.84 is a reasonable benchmark to which we may compare our persistence estimates.

3.2.2 Are Aggregate Perceptions of Parties Time-Stable?

With a within-individual benchmark for perception stability in hand, we now investigate the stability in the aggregate. We begin by analyzing the British placements for Labour, Liberal Democrats, Conservatives, and UKIP from the Sophia data. We plot the Sophia *perceptions* in Figure 5 for the four parties from 12 surveys across 1983–2019.

Meaningful shifts *do* occur – both the Labour Party and Conservatives experience centrist shifts in perceptions in the 1990s, and UKIP makes a strong tack to the right following the deposition of leader Alan Sked in 1997 by a contingent led by Nigel Farage, and again after Farage himself won formal control in 2006. More generally, British party brands are characterized by considerable stability in this period. Perceptions remain in their ideological neighborhoods, and changes to the ideological rank ordering are driven by fledgling, minor parties bouncing around their more stable, mainstream counterparts (Budge 1994).

Given the stability depicted in Figure 5, we expect a high rate of persistence to formally manifest in a regression model. Table 6 shows the persistence level

Table 6 *Autoregressive Distributed Lag* (1;0) results of the aggregate persistence in British parties from 1983–2019

	Survey means	**Sophia**
Perceptions$_{t-1}$	0.95*	0.88*
	(0.07)	(0.08)
Constant	0.34	0.71
	(0.37)	(0.41)
N	44	44
Adjusted R^2	0.81	0.74

Note: *: p-value < 0.05

in perceptions – measured by the coefficient of the lagged dependent variable – for both survey means (first column) and Sophia (second column).

Both persistence rates are quite high, which suggests that shocks to perceptions tend to be small in the short term but reverberate with time as the series progresses. In both models, prior perceptions explain a great deal of the variance in current perceptions, as shown by the adjusted R^2 values. These values suggest that any model specification of party perceptions should therefore recognize the high rate of persistence and the need for a lagged dependent variable – especially given that theoretical arguments are nearly all focused on *change* in perceptions. Note that the persistence rate for the survey means is much larger than the rate from the Sophia model and indeed overlaps 1. We cannot say for certain why this is the case, but this estimate strikes us as incredibly high, in part because an estimate of 1 is prima facia incredible – we know qualitatively that brand perceptions do change – and in part because the persistence rate for the Sophia model (0.88) is much closer to the benchmark persistence uncovered in the individual-level UK data (0.84), indicating that Sophia is a better approximation of within-individual persistence, which we would consider a gold standard for studying maintenance and change in party perceptions. Relative to Sophia, in this case, survey means underestimate the degree to which perceptions of parties may change from one period to the next. This may suggest that survey means are also likely to underestimate the responsiveness of voter perceptions to party events, such as the issuance of a new platform or the formation of a new government. We also note, however, that survey means do not always have a higher persistence rate in country-level subsamples. For example, persistence for means is higher than Sophia in Denmark and the UK, lower in Austria and Iceland, and indifferentiable in the Netherlands. The differences are idiosyncratic, just as the aggregation of differing respondents with differing nonresponse propensities, and differing relationships to parties is idiosyncratic.

We derive two lessons – one theoretical and one empirical – from this exploration. First, party brand stability at the party level has its roots in individual stability. This is consistent with our theoretical framework for understanding voters' perceptions as distributions of party-related messages connoting policy preferences that change through the incorporation of new messages based on their cost, credibility, and salience. Second, the exploration provides empirical justification for a statistical specification that appropriately models the autoregressive nature of party brands. The best predictor of *current* perceptions is *prior* perceptions, whether at the individual or party level. Importantly, this empirical specification is not just concordant with our theoretical framework, but indeed suggested by it. An important caveat to this, however, is that the persistence estimate should be statistically and substantively less than 1, allowing for perceptions to be appropriately responsive to new events and information. We believe that the panel-data derived estimate of 0.84 is a reasonable benchmark. At 0.84, perceptions are sticky – where yesterday's draw accounts for roughly five-sixths of today's draw – but still reliably incorporate information from recent events. The central remaining choice is whether and how to model concurrent and lagged values of the predictors.

3.2.3 Model Specification of Stability and Change

To test our hypotheses regarding durability and change in voters' perceptions of party brands, we utilize an *Autoregressive Distributed Lag* model or ADL, the appropriate specification for assessing the short- and long-term effects of the covariates for a persistent series (for examples, see Adams, Ezrow, and Somer-Topcu 2011, 2014):

$$Y_{pt} = \alpha_0 + \alpha_1 Y_{pt-1} + \beta_0 \mathbf{X}_{pt} + \beta_1 \mathbf{X}_{pt-1} + \epsilon_{pt} \tag{1}$$

With minimal rearrangement, this model specification allows us extract all values of interest necessary to understand the durability of perceptions and the short- and long-term effects of different covariates. As discussed, the degree of persistence (or the carry-over of perceptions from one period to the next) is α_1, the short-run effect of concurrent values of covariate vector $\mathbf{X}_{pt}$ is captured by β_0, the short-run effect of past values of covariates $\mathbf{X}_{pt-1}$ is β_1, and the total effect of these covariates, given their persistence on past and present realizations of the dependent variable, which is called the "long-run multiplier" of $\mathbf{X}$, is $\frac{\beta_0 + \beta_1}{(1 - \alpha_1)}$.

The ADL is general enough that we can test restrictions that previous studies have implicitly imposed on their data. This helps address a common problem identified in De Boef and Keele's (2008, p. 184) seminal piece of temporal dynamics: "Analysts tend to adopt restrictive dynamic specifications on the basis of limited theoretical guidance and without empirical evidence that restrictions are valid, potentially biasing inferences and invalidating hypothesis tests." Simple t-tests or F-tests, coupled with theoretical guidance, can direct scholars to the appropriate dynamic specification, but here, we walk through the substantive effects of these choices to better illustrate analysts' choices.

Take, for example, the specification De Boef and Keele (2008) call a *"Static"* model, which has been used in several studies of party perceptions:

$$Y_{pt} = \alpha_0 + \beta_0 \mathbf{X}_{pt} + \epsilon_{pt} \tag{2}$$

Equation 2 assumes that Equation 1's parameters $\alpha_1 = \beta_1 = 0$. Our theoretical and qualitative understanding of how voters' perceptions of parties are formed and updated suggests these assumptions are untrue. For example, in the case of how the public responds to campaign statements, the assumption that $\alpha_1 = \beta_1 = 0$ means that a change in advertised positions at time t is felt *immediately* and *completely* at time t, and, evaporates *entirely* by time $t+1$ – in other words, that specification constrains voters to have no memory of previous positions and therefore also constrains party positions to be completely malleable from one period to the next. We have just demonstrated these assumptions to be untrue. Further, because we know the lagged dependent variable is a strong predictor of the current value, *and*, because our theoretical understanding of voters' perceptions tells us that that relationship is *causal*, failing to include the lagged DV will induce omitted variable bias if it is in any way correlated with included predictors. This is likely, and more so if some of the covariates (such as party positions) are themselves autoregressive. As a result, in practice, estimates of short- or long-term effects will be biased and the errors are likely to be positively autocorrelated, which results in standard error estimates that are too small. As a consequence, scholars may make incorrect inferences about the size of contemporaneous effects and may be prone to rejecting true null hypotheses.

There are many other specifications apart from the ADL and static model (De Boef and Keele 2008). A more popular model (e.g., Fernandez-Vazquez and Somer-Topcu 2019) is the *"Partial Adjustment"* model, in Equation 3, which allows for persistent effects by including the lagged dependent variable, but imposes the constraint that $\beta_1 = 0$.

$$Y_{pt} = \alpha_0 + \alpha_1 Y_{pt-1} + \beta_0 \mathbf{X}_{pt} + \epsilon_{pt} \tag{3}$$

This specification allows a covariate to have an immediate, short-term effect on Y_t and then a persistent, long-term effect through its impact on the lagged dependent variable; however, there is no lagged effect of X_{t-1} on Y_t. In more substantive terms, this specification restricts the impact of events on voters' perceptions to be immediate *only*. In the case of, say, government formation, this means that voters must extract whatever policy signals from the formation of the government and incorporate them today, but cannot extract and incorporate information from this event tomorrow. If this restriction is violated in reality, then both β_0 and α_1 are biased. Importantly, if the researcher does not know the nature of the autocorrelation in **X**, then they cannot know the nature of the bias induced to estimates in β_0 and α_1, and their standard errors, due to this specification choice.

Like the *Partial Adjustment* model, each of the other specifications, in one way or another, imposes constraints on effect manifestation that our understanding of the process suggests are unrealistic.

$$Y_{pt} = \alpha_0 + \alpha_1 Y_{pt-1} + \beta_1 \mathbf{X}_{pt-1} + \epsilon_{pt} \tag{4}$$

For example, the "*Dead Start*" specification, in Equation 4, allows for the interpretation of long-term effects, but does not allow covariates to have an immediate effect on the outcome, which we know is unlikely to be accurate for most relevant events. If there is positive covariance between X_t and X_{t-1}, then the estimate of β_1 will be biased upward.

Our review of previous studies of voters' perceptions of party brands reveals pronounced and pervasive disagreement over model specifications. De Boef and Keele (2008, p. 185) find similar trends for time series models in general between 1995 and 2005: "Our review suggests not only that restrictive models are prevalent, but also that dynamic specifications are often selected ad hoc. In particular, frequently there is no discussion on the decision to include contemporaneous values of the exogenous variables as opposed to (or in addition to) lagged values." These decisions are particularly problematic when the authors present no evidence in favor of their restrictions, or when the theoretical basis for the imposed restrictions is lacking (De Boef and Keele 2008, pp.185–186).

Our theoretical framework implies a dynamic process for both outcome and predictor, such that the voter perceptions of party brands should be modeled with an ADL (1;1) specification (at least for the mean of the distribution; we discuss the variance in Section 4). Even if our theoretical model was agnostic over dynamics, the data are not. Given the observed durability of party perceptions over time, the consistency of party pronouncements in campaigns and pursuits in government, and the loyalty of party supporters, we know that strict assumptions on dynamics of the sort imposed by the static model are simply unacceptable. Importantly, empirical specifications formalize *unbreakable theoretical assumptions* and lock them into the estimation process, limiting the range of relationships allowed to manifest. Estimating an ADL, which facilitates both contemporaneous and lagged effects in the context of persistent outcomes, frees us from these unrealistic and strict restrictions.

3.2.4 Sensitivity to Specification

To illustrate how the inferences change depending on the model specification, we walk through several different specifications for a simple model estimating party placement with one predictor: that party's stated policy goals as derived from its campaign manifestos (*manifesto position*). This model is simply an illustrative exercise. It does not reflect our theoretical predictions regarding the impact of government participation on voters' perceptions, nor does it include additional sources of uncertainty. However, it is helpful in clearly illustrating how simple choices in modeling the dynamics of the series result in meaningful differences in the conclusions one is able to make.

We estimate our illustrative model with five dynamic specifications using the Sophia measure from the Sophia data: the *Autoregressive Distributed Lag* (ADL) model, which includes lagged and concurrent values of *manifesto position*; the *Partial Adjustment* model, which includes concurrent values of all independent variables and a lagged dependent variable; the *Dead Start* model, which includes lags of all independent variables and a lagged dependent variable; the *Finite Distributed Lag* model, which includes concurrent values and lags of the independent variables alone; and the *Static* model, which includes concurrent values of the independent variables.

We first calculate the short- (STE) and long-term effects (LTE) of *manifesto positions* as well as the persistence rate of *perceptions*. A complete interpretation of these values is necessary to understand persistent effects. For example, consider the *Partial Adjustment* model proposed by Fernandez-Vazquez and Somer-Topcu (2019, p. 10). The authors note that the small effect of *manifesto position* on voter perceptions (0.08), in combination with the high degree of persistence in the *lagged perceptions* (0.91), means that "the left–right party image that emerges after the campaign is largely driven by initial voter beliefs." This is a correct interpretation, but the conclusion that election campaigns have a "substantively small" effect on perceptions is not. The difference is in focusing on the STE – which is quite small (0.08) – while neglecting the LTE *manifesto position* – which is more than 10 times the magnitude (0.89), but can only be learned by deriving the sustained impact of concurrent changes in X, though its persistent effects on future values of Y through Y_{t-1}. In this case, the high degree of persistence in *perceptions* means that short-term perturbations will tend to be small, but will be long-lasting as the series returns to its equilibrium.

Figure 6 displays the persistence rates of *perceptions*, STEs, and LTEs derived from each of these models. Hollow circles on the zero line denote effects that are restricted to be 0 by model construction, and by extension theoretical assumption. In all five specifications, there is a strong and substantively meaningful impact of manifesto positions on perceptions; the total effects of *positions* – LTEs in the first three models and the summed effects in the last two models – exceed 1.0. This means that in this simple illustrative model, changes in positions are completely incorporated into *perceptions* over a finite number of periods. The difference, however, is whether these effects are incorporated immediately (*Static*), in the first two periods (*Finite Distributed Lag*), or indefinitely. These are not irrelevant differences; they bear important theoretical and substantive implications. Further, critically, if the results uncovered by the *Static* model reflected the "true" process, then those results would also be manifest in the ADL, which would reveal estimates of persistence, STE of *manifesto position*, and STE of *lagged manifesto position* of 0. This is not the case. The *Static* model incorrectly leads us to the interpretation that *manifesto positions* are digested and incorporated in their entirety in a single interval as a function of the positive covariance of *manifesto positions* with the omitted lags of outcome and predictor. We know this covariance because we have composed this study and estimated all models, but in everyday practice, researchers may not estimate all models and consumers of the research have no way of immediately evaluating these factors. As such, we argue that estimation of an ADL specification is appropriate in more or less all applications, because it imposes no ex ante constraints on the ability of true STEs or LTEs to manifest in estimation. This property is best illustrated comparing ADL to *Partial Adjustment*, which constrains the STE of lagged *manifesto positions* to 0 by assumption. In this particular case, the ADL also recovers a 0 estimate on that value. By happenstance, *Partial Adjustment* recovers the "true" value of quantities of interest, but, again, we only know this in this case because we have estimated all constructions.

A final note on interpretation. At first glance, the LTEs appear to be quite large: A 1-unit shift to the right in *manifesto position* in the ADL model results in an LTE effect of nearly a 1.4-unit shift to the right in *perceptions*. Substantively, this means that respondents (eventually) fully incorporate platform changes into their perceived placements of that party. While the combined STEs are smaller (0.20), the high persistence in *perceptions* results in additional effects that decline slowly (86%) for a long period.

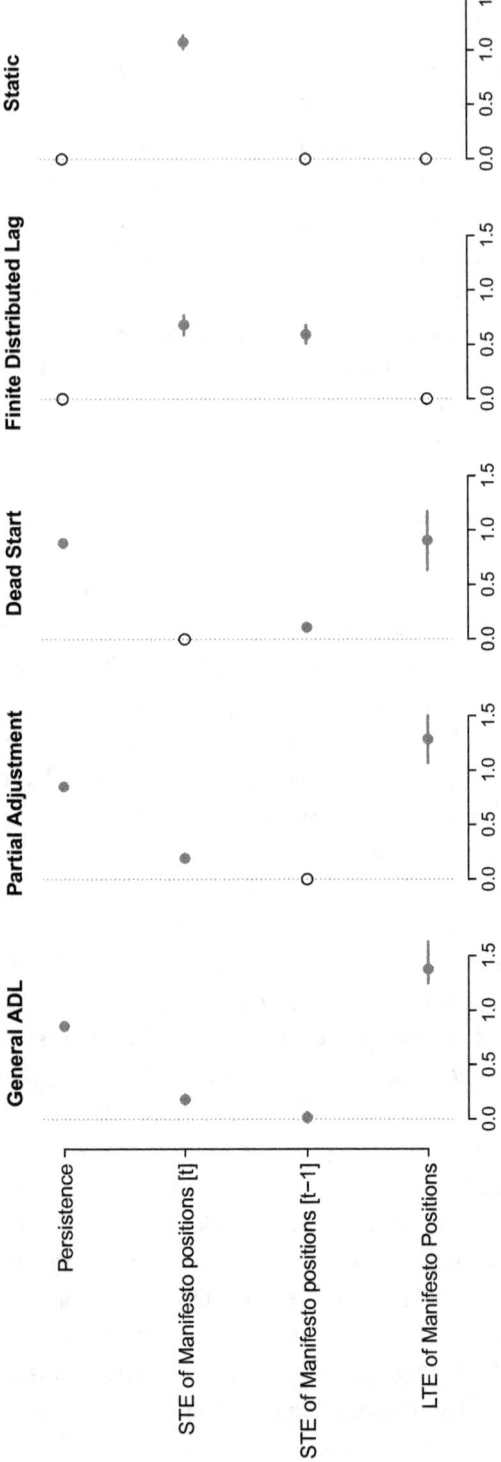

Figure 6 Illustration of the persistence and effects of *positions* across dynamic model specifications.

In practice, however, the LTEs of *manifesto positions* on *perceptions* are unlikely to be that large. Long-term effects illustrate the total effects of *manifesto positions* in a vacuum, simulated out to infinity. This relies on the ceteris paribus assumption, which is not realistic when discussing elections held every few years – voters (and parties) only live so long. More importantly, the world is not stable enough to observe anything close to the estimated infinite LTE. Circumstances that previously influenced strategy change from one period to the next. Governments are formed, dissolved, and replaced with new coalitions (Fortunato and Stevenson 2013a). Electoral results inform parties about the wisdom of their strategically selected campaign platforms and parties update accordingly (Somer-Topcu 2009). For these reasons, we think a more realistic depiction of the total effects of *positions* focuses on dynamic simulations over relatively few periods rather than an LTE that we are unlikely to ever fully observe (Williams and Whitten 2012).

Figure 7 depicts the effect of a one-unit increase (move to the right) of *positions* at time t for four time intervals, across the five dynamic specifications. This is one or two more time units than we would recommend scholars interpret in their own research; we model the effects farther into the future to show just how drastically the total effect estimates vary. In all five specifications, we conclude with a high degree of confidence that *manifesto positions* and *perceptions* are positively linked, but the five specifications tell different stories about the timing of the effects and their overall size. The ADL and *Partial Adjustment* models are quite similar both in the size of the effects at each period and their pattern of decay because the estimates from ADL are very consistent with the estimated *and* constrained coefficients from the *Partial Adjustment* model. As just discussed, this is because, in this case, the "true" process is recovered by *Partial Adjustment* and this is manifest in the ADL recovering a 0 estimate on the STE of lagged *manifesto positions*, which can be seen in Figure 6 and the striking similarity of the effect estimates plotted in Figure 7.

The remaining three specifications impose modeling restrictions that are not borne out in the data. The result is inferences that have little support in reality. Take, for example, the *Dead Start* model, which omits the concurrent effect of *manifesto positions*. Substantively, this means that voters ignore the barrage of election-related political messages while they are happening, but incorporate them with a lag of one election. Each period's effects are smaller than those in the ADL or *Partial Adjustment* models and the total effect across all periods (0.286) is less than half of what is estimated by the ADL. There is no persistence in either the *Finite Distributed Lag* or *Static* models, so the entire effect of *manifesto positions* must occur at either the first two periods (if a lag is included) or in the first period (*Static*). As De Boef and Keele (2008) show, bias

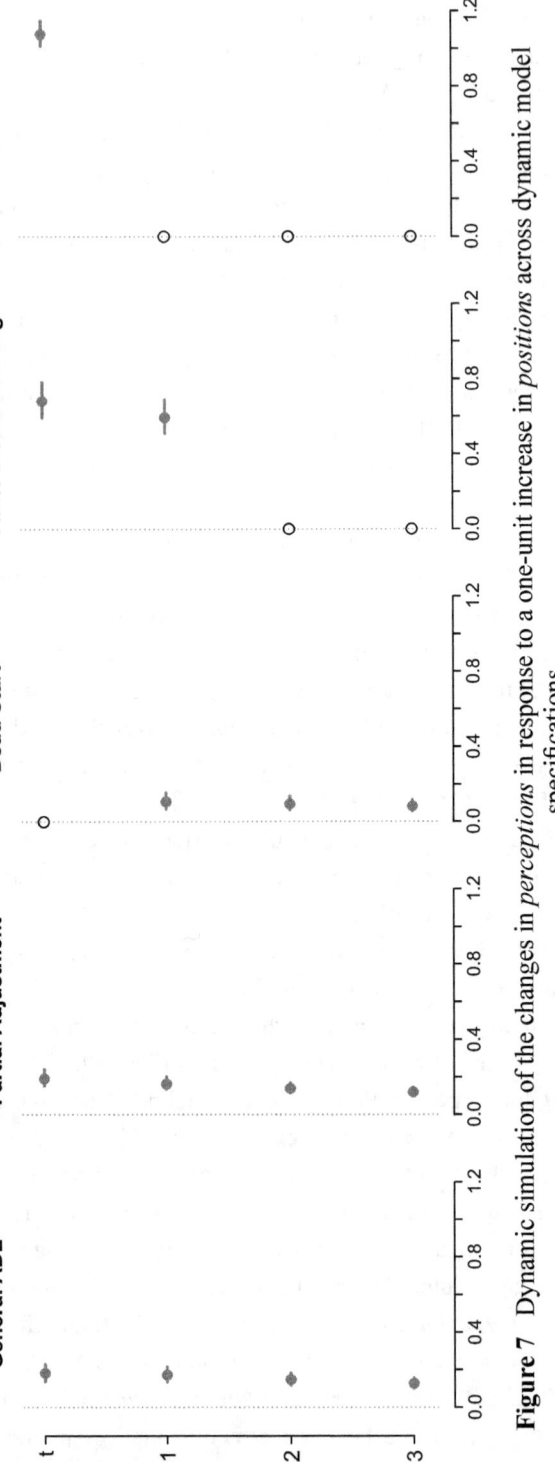

Figure 7 Dynamic simulation of the changes in *perceptions* in response to a one-unit increase in *positions* across dynamic model specifications.

in coefficients will be larger at greater lag lengths; in this case, the more durable party brands are, the greater the bias in the relationship between *manifesto positions* and *perceptions*. The estimates reflect this bias. The *Finite Distributed Lag* model estimates a total effect of 1.276 and the *Static* model estimates a total effect of 1.075; both are about twice the ADL estimate.

These models produce estimated effect timings and sizes that are categorical departures from both the properly estimated effect and our qualitative understanding of the underlying processes. Importantly, we reiterate, if the constraints these models place on covariates by assumption held in reality, the ADL would recover them. That is, if the *Finite Distributed Lag* model, which constrains persistence to 0 by omitting a lagged dependent variable, was "correct," the ADL would reflect this and recover a 0 estimate on the lag of the outcome. Of course, there is an efficiency trade-off to the ADL; it requires more parameters than all other specifications, including double the parameters of the *Static* model. But in practice this is a trade worth making, particularly if researchers are using our Sophia data, which have about 10 times the power of the typical sample analyzed in our survey of the extant literature.

3.2.5 Modeling Uncertainty

Our final consideration addresses measurement error in covariates, an integral part of the analytical process that almost every study has disregarded. Our two central measures are estimates with associated uncertainty properties. Our Sophia estimates contain uncertainty from the imputation algorithm, uncertainty from the estimated relationships between respondent characteristics and their perceptions of each party, and, of course, survey respondents' underlying uncertainty about where any particular party is located in the policy space. These are all "baked in" to our 1,000 Sophia estimates for each survey party. Our focal covariate, party platforms as derived from codings of campaign manifestos, also have associated uncertainty properties. Those properties are discussed at some length by Benoit, Laver, and Mikhaylov (2009), Lowe et al. (2011), and others, and include inter-coder reliability, the clarity of signal in the document (or number of reinforcing statements relative to potentially contradictory statements), and the aggregate number of clear policy statements made. This error, if not incorporated into our statistical models, could bias results. We would almost certainly underestimate the standard errors on the parameters of interest and we may also misestimate parameters, particularly if the errors are correlated with other covariates, which we believe is likely.

We suggest modeling the error in these variables by bootstrapping, which we demonstrate in Section 4. For covariates derived from Sophia, we iterate through each of our 1,000 Sophia draws for each survey party. For manifesto-derived covariates, we specify a normal distribution following Lowe et al. (2011), where the distribution mean is a function of the logged ratio of right-to-left policy statements ($\mu = log\frac{R+0.5}{L+0.5}$) and the variance is proportional the sum of inverted counts of right and left policy statements ($\sigma^2 = (R + 0.5)^{-1} + (L + 0.5)^{-1}$). We then specify and estimate our statistical model for each of our 1,000 Sophia draws, resampling our manifesto covariates from their distributions for each iteration, and recording 100 posterior samples of the estimated parameters following King, Tomz, and Wittenberg (2000). This results in a vector of 100,000 draws for each estimated parameter, representing the cumulative uncertainty of estimated relationships and the measurement error in the data from which those relationships are estimated. We use this approach in Section 4 to test our hypotheses.

4 Putting It All Together

In this section, we combine our theoretical framework, data, and dynamic modeling suggestions to derive and test new hypotheses on how voters generate and update their perceptions of parties' policy brands. In keeping with the previous discussion of the theoretical framework, our efforts here will primarily focus on just two event types – government formation and the content of electoral manifestos. This focus will allow us to forego much discussion on the cost, credibility, and salience of the associated policy information, as we have already completed a great deal of that exercise. Unlike the previous discussion, however, we will discuss one party characteristic, two event characteristics, and one system-level characteristic, rather than just parties' status as cabinet or opposition. Also, we push our discussion beyond the first moment (μ) of brand perceptions to think through potential implications for the variance (σ^2) of voters' party perceptions.

4.1 Empirical Expectations

To review, we assume that voters use a spatial metaphor to organize the policy preferences of relevant political actors, such as parties and cabinets. We further assume that this organizing space is unidimensional, where policy preferences across the complete array of policy jurisdictions can be coarsened to a point on that continuum. Finally, we assume that the general orientation of the unidimensional space is more or less consistent within a given context, such that most voters and elites agree what constitutes a "left" or a "right" position on most issues. Generalizing from Zaller (1992), we consider voters' perceptions of parties to be realizations $y \in (L, R)$ of a normally distributed random variable $Y \sim N(\mu, \sigma^2)$.[17] As noted earlier, this structure allows us to estimate the likelihood of the distribution's governing parameters given the observation of a particular vector of the random variable $L(\mu, \sigma^2 \mid Y = y)$, which of course can be modeled statistically with covariates. That is, we can measure observable characteristics of parties that would lead voters to perceive them as more left or right and model μ with those characteristics. Likewise, we can measure observable characteristics of parties that would lead voters to perceive them with more or less variability and model σ^2 with those characteristics. This is the focus of the section.

Focusing on μ, in Section 2 we derived the following hypotheses for how cabinet formation and campaign platforms should affect voters' perceptions of cabinet and opposition parties:

μ_1 Perceptions of coalition parties are positively correlated with perceptions of their partners in government.

μ_2 Perceptions of opposition parties are negatively correlated with perceptions of the government.

μ_3 Policy programs are positively incorporated into voters' perceptions.

μ_4 Perceptions of opposition parties are more heavily influenced by policy programs than cabinet parties.

How might cabinet formation and campaign platforms affect the *variance* of voters' perceptions? We argue that government participation should decrease the uncertainty (σ^2) of voters' perceptions, not because the policy information transmitted by cabinet information is likely to be more consistent – we already discussed how cabinet parties' records of governance compete with their campaign platforms – but simply because there is more of it. Most cabinets enjoy a monopoly on proposal power and set the parliamentary agenda, and, each submission or passage of a cabinet proposal is a relevant news event. Cabinet parties also possess greater speaking time in the plenary (Bäck et al. 2019), command attention in their executive (bureaucratic) capacity, and are, in general, the public face of government both domestically and globally. Each of these factors leads cabinet parties to dominate media coverage of politics relative to their opposition counterparts (Baumgartner and Chaqués Bonafont 2015). That is, all of the information conveyed by cabinet participation (and potentially electoral manifestos) is more *available* for cabinet parties such that

---

[17] Where L and R are arbitrarily small and large bounds on $\mathbb{R}$ representing the leftmost and rightmost policy position.

voters are receiving fewer draws from the "true distribution" of opposition parties' policy activities. Our expectation, therefore, is that the variance (σ^2) in voters' perceptions of cabinet parties will be less than the variance in voters' perceptions of opposition parties.

Campaign platforms should also have a strong effect on voters' perceptions by exhibiting greater or lesser degrees of clarity and stability.[18] Manifestos that hedge or take coarse or ambiguous positions may leave voters uncertain about what parties' true policy objectives are, leading to greater variance (σ^2) in voters' perceptions of the parties' brands. That is, holding constant that the information in the manifesto is made available, credible, and salient, the clarity of the policy positions communicated by that document (or via media and party leadership) should determine the clarity with which the party brand is perceived.

Related, large changes to platforms from one election to the next should similarly increase voters' uncertainty (σ^2) over where a party stands for at least three reasons. First, sustained and persistent messaging is more likely to produce clear and consistent signals than messages that vary widely over time. Second, substantial temporal changes in position may induce aggregate variability through individualized temporal differences in attentiveness – people who were not paying attention yesterday will possess different information than people who were not paying attention today. Third, large changes may be viewed as less credible, either because they are discordant with voters' prior or because they made be viewed as cheap talk. Related, though there are intuitive short-term incentives for parties to "chase" voters (e.g., Laver 2005), the preponderance of theoretical research emphasizes strong long-term incentives toward stability, not the least of which is the value of positional consistency in maintaining credibility and enabling clear communication (Enelow and Hinich 1984; Budge 1994; Aldrich 1995). Our expectation is that greater changes in manifesto position from one election to the next will lead to greater variance (σ^2) in voters' perceptions of the parties' brands.

We now turn to context. Voters' perceptions of parties are especially relevant in the shadow of an election when they are preparing to make their vote choice, but in our sample of Europe's parliamentary countries voters evaluate

---

[18] Of course, there could be strategic reasons for differences here. For example, Tomz and Van Houweling (2009) and Somer-Topcu (2015) argue that parties may be incentivized toward making ambiguous policy pronouncements in order to let voters see what they prefer to see in the campaign statements, though the benefits of this strategy may be limited by the voters' ability to distinguish the ideologies of rival parties Shin and Williams (2024).

the same parties in their competition for both the national and European legislature. Voters' perceptions of a given party should exhibit lower uncertainty (σ^2) about national elections relative to European elections. This is because European parliamentary elections are simply less important to a broad swath of the electorate than national elections; they are "second-order" elections, decided on the same dimensions as national elections, but by a much smaller and more politically interested portion of the electorate (Reif and Schmitt 1980; Hobolt and Wittrock 2011; Söderlund, Wass, and Blais 2011).[19] This implies lower general attentiveness, such that party messaging around European elections will be less available (as a function of lowered demand for news coverage), collected by a smaller number of voters, and less salient than messaging around national elections. This depressed availability, attentiveness, and salience should depress overall acquisition of the policy information we have been discussing here and in Section 2, driving greater variance (σ^2) of voters' perceptions around European elections relative to national elections. This leaves us with the following ceteris paribus empirical expectations:

σ_1^2 Variance in perceptions will be smaller for cabinet parties than opposition parties.
σ_2^2 Variance in perceptions will be greater when variance in policy programs is greater.
σ_3^2 Variance in perceptions will be greater when change in policy programs is greater.
σ_4^2 Variance in perceptions will be greater about European elections than national elections.

Zooming out, more generally, we suspect that the nature of opinion formation will make observing large changes to perceived positions (μ) unlikely, as we alluded to in Section 3. There are several reasons for this. First, the opinion model suggests that if the information that is incorporated into voters' perceptual distributions is at all durable (i.e., the information does not evaporate or get displaced immediately), then these perceptions should be stable over time as it would take a great deal of new information implying a different position to significantly alter μ.[20] Second, there is a short supply of credible actions

---

[19] Indeed, content analysis of media coverage of EP elections even shows that when the elections are covered, focus is much more often on domestic issues and actors than European issues and actors (De Vreese et al. 2006).

[20] Our empirical approach is flexible to different assumptions, or testing of empirical expectations, regarding information decay and we believe that may be an interesting subject of study in future research.

parties can take to send those differentiating signals outside of election campaigns (when political attention is high) and outside of their participation in government.[21] Third, as just mentioned, parties have strong incentives to craft and maintain stable positions, even if a particular position is not preferred by a plurality of voters. There is a fair amount of theoretical and empirical evidence that parties are reticent to drastically change their positions, precisely because they believe consistency breeds credibility. Not only does positional stability clarify signals to voters regarding what a party wants, but it may also increase the party's "valence" in the eyes of the electorate (e.g., Aldrich 1995; Adams 2001).

Outside political science, marketing scholars concur on the importance of brand stability in competitive marketplaces, generally concluding that stability reduces perceived risk on the part of the consumer and helps build brand loyalty, which combine to present a higher (perceived) relative value to consumers (e.g., Leischnig and Enke 2011). The clear analogue is that parties with stable, consistent policy offerings reduce uncertainty over what they may do in government while also building loyalty in the electorate through reliable messaging and, hopefully, delivering on their policy promises when in government. Indeed, cartel theory – perhaps the most influential model of legislative organization – is entirely motivated by party members' collective acceptance that their brand is a valuable common good that must be protected. The authors use this language explicitly – "parties compete in mass elections, as firms compete in mass markets, by developing brand names" (Cox and McCubbins 2005, p. 32).

Our general expectation, then, is that perceptions of party brands will be fairly consistent over time, but this is not strictly speaking a falsifiable hypothesis, as we would have to choose some (arbitrary) value of the estimated persistence. That is, we can assess whether persistence is positive or not, or, following recent legislative research, assess the probability that the estimate falls within a particular interval (Provins, Monroe, and Fortunato 2022). But our theoretical understanding of persistence is insufficiently precise to derive a particular point or interval expectation. Our best guess for what aggregate persistence should be is the persistence we estimated from BES panel data in Section 3 (0.84), so we will use this figure as our benchmark and assess proximity to it as an indication that our model is well calibrated and our theoretical understanding of brand stability is reasonable.[22]

---

[21] See Fortunato (2021) and Adams, Weschle, and Wlezien (2021) for more discussion on this.
[22] We suspect that this estimate may be slightly inflated given that the benchmark excludes nonresponders and attriters, both of whom have less consistent and stable political opinions.

4.2 Statistical Model

Our theoretical framework and hypotheses call for a model that will allow us to simultaneously estimate the effects of observable characteristics of parties (or their events, etc.) that shape μ and σ^2, the first and second moments of a (normal) random variable. We observe voters' perceptions of parties p at times t, and regress those perceptions y_{pt} on matrices of observable characteristics of parties $\mathbf{X}$ and $\mathbf{Z}$ – the manifesto position, cabinet participation, etc. – in the following framework:

$$y_{pt} = \beta \mathbf{X}_{pt} + \varepsilon_{pt}, \qquad (5)$$

where, $\varepsilon_{pt} \sim N(0, \sigma^2_{pt})$,

$$\sigma^2_{pt} = \exp(\gamma \mathbf{Z}_{pt}), \qquad (6)$$

In other words, we want to simultaneously find the candidate values of $\hat{\beta}$ and $\hat{\gamma}$, the vector of coefficient weights placed on covariate matrices $\mathbf{X}$ and $\mathbf{Z}$, that maximize the probability of observing of the voters' perceptions of parties recorded in our data, $\mathrm{pr}(Y = y \mid \mu = \hat{\beta}\mathbf{X}, \sigma^2 = \exp(\hat{\gamma}\mathbf{Z}))$. We can solve Equations 5 and 6 simultaneously by maximizing the log-likelihood function given in Equation 7:

$$\ln L(\hat{\beta}, \hat{\gamma} \mid y) = \sum_{p=1, t=1}^{P,T} \left\{ -\frac{1}{2} \ln(2\pi) - \frac{1}{2} \hat{\gamma} \mathbf{Z}_{pt} - \frac{1}{2\exp(\hat{\gamma}\mathbf{Z}_{pt})} (y_{pt} - \hat{\beta}\mathbf{X}_{pt})^2 \right\} \qquad (7)$$

Such models are typically referred to as "conditionally heteroskedastic" models, as they model the conditional variance in the data, rather than the unconditional variance as in, for example, Ezrow (2007) or Ezrow, Homola, and Tavits (2014), which regress variance estimates on covariates, separate from the means of the underlying distributions. These models are somewhat rare in political science, though not at all unheard of; see for instance, King (1989), Alvarez and Brehm (1995), or Williams and Brule (2014). Our specification includes an *Autoregressive Distributed Lag* (ADL) construction in the mean portion, allowing us to estimate both short- and long-term effects of party actions on voters' perceptions of their positions and the persistence (or durability) of voters' perceptions of party locations over time, as discussed in Section 3. Our conditional variance specification includes concurrent values of the covariates, allowing us to estimate the immediate effect of party characteristics on the predictability of voters' perceptions, given the short- and long-term directional effects.[23]

The mean portion of the model, constructed to test $\mu_1:\mu_4$, contains positional estimates from the focal party's manifesto calculated according to Lowe et al. (2011) as we discussed in Section 3. The model also includes the government's position. Where the focal party is in opposition, the measure is the perceived position of the entire cabinet, and where the focal party is in the cabinet, it is the perceived position of the focal party's *coalition partners*. Both cabinet position estimates are the seat-weighted average position of the parties, the standard estimate in comparative politics, as seen in Powell (2000), Martin and Vanberg (2011), Fortunato (2021), and many others. We include concurrent and lagged values of both manifesto and cabinet positions. The focal party's manifesto position is interacted with an indicator for its cabinet participation, and the cabinet's position is interacted with an indicator for whether the focal party is a member of a *coalition* cabinet.[24] This coalition indicator allows the model to differentiate between focal parties that are part of coalition governments – that is, cabinet parties that have partners in government, which should affect how they are perceived – and focal parties that govern alone – that is, cabinet parties without partners in government, which should not affect how they are perceived.

To test $\sigma_1^2:\sigma_4^2$, we include in the variance portion of the model an indicator for government (relative to opposition) status, the estimated uncertainty of the parties' manifesto positions, the change in the parties' positions from the previous contest, and a dummy indicating whether the survey was administered for a European (relative to national) parliamentary election. Manifesto uncertainty is captured by the standard error of the parties' manifesto position, and manifesto change is the absolute difference between the current and previous manifesto position. Both manifesto positions and standard errors are calculated (as before) following Lowe et al. (2011). We also include two potential confounders, party seat share and party age, both of which may simultaneously predict perception

---

[23] Diagnostics reveal that the conditional variance does not have the same kind of durable memory as the distribution mean, indicating that autoregressive approaches to modeling the variance may not be necessary to obtain unbiased estimates. Including lags of the covariates more or less just splits the explanatory power between lagged and concurrent values (with more on the concurrent) as a function of their observed covariance. That said, there is no reason for researchers *not* to employ such a strategy if their theoretical framework suggested an autoregressive process.

[24] The cabinet position covariate takes on a value of 0 when the focal party is governing alone. Such observations represent about 7% of our sample.

Table 7 Model estimation results for mean and variance of party perceptions

	Covariate	Mean	SD	p
μ	Perceptions$_{t-1}$	0.843	(0.014)	0.000
	Government	−0.027	(0.128)	0.417
	Coalition partner	−0.726	(0.174)	0.000
	Cabinet ideology	−0.037	(0.019)	0.025
	Manifesto position	0.154	(0.039)	0.000
	Government$_{t-1}$	−0.225	(0.130)	0.041
	Coalition partner$_{t-1}$	0.127	(0.180)	0.240
	Cabinet ideology$_{t-1}$	−0.031	(0.019)	0.044
	Manifesto position$_{t-1}$	0.022	(0.035)	0.263
	Coalition partner × Cabinet ideology	0.161	(0.034)	0.000
	Coalition partner$_{t-1}$ × Cabinet ideology$_{t-1}$	0.007	(0.035)	0.427
	Government × Manifesto position	−0.074	(0.053)	0.079
	Government$_{t-1}$ × Manifesto position$_{t-1}$	0.007	(0.052)	0.448
	Intercept	1.186	(0.142)	0.000
σ^2	Government	−0.102	(0.060)	0.040
	Manifesto uncertainty	0.460	(0.234)	0.030
	Manifesto change	0.047	(0.049)	0.167
	European election	0.238	(0.047)	0.000
	Seat share	−0.119	(0.182)	0.258
	Party age	−0.108	(0.026)	0.000
	Intercept	−0.299	(0.112)	0.004
	N	1329		
	log(likelihood)	−1,296.079		

Note: Dependent variable includes estimates of voters' placements of parties (Sophia). p = directional probabilities

variability and governing status. We take these covariates from Volkens et al. (2017).[25]

Our estimation sample is restricted to 32 parliamentary systems: Australia, Austria, Belgium, Canada, Croatia, Czech Republic, Denmark, Estonia, Finland, Germany, Greece, Hungary, Iceland, Ireland, Israel, Italy, Japan, Latvia, Lithuania, Luxembourg, Malta, the Netherlands, New Zealand, Norway,

---

[25] We use the publication date of a party's earliest manifesto to calculate its age.

Poland, Portugal, Romania, Slovakia, Slovenia, Spain, Sweden, and the United Kingdom.

The final sample includes 269 parties, observed between 2 and 21 times, in 46 unique years between 1965 and 2019, summing to a total of $n = 1,329$ (note that we lose one observation of each party by including lagged covariates). As discussed in Section 3, we account for measurement uncertainty in outcome and predictor as well as uncertainty related to imputation. We combine the imputed datasets and then bootstrap estimation, resampling estimates of focal party perceptions, government position, manifesto position, and manifesto change 1,000 times, and aggregate bootstrapped estimates via posterior sampling following Tomz, Wittenberg, and King (2001). These estimates therefore include two sources of uncertainty typically neglected in analyses of voters' placements.

Full model results are shown in Table 7, including directional probabilities for all estimates, which can be interpreted as typical one-tailed p values. Recall that the outcome is our estimate of voters' placements of parties based on the Sophia archetype.

4.3 Results

To test hypotheses $\mu_1:\mu_4$, we calculate the short- and long-term effects of cabinet ideology and focal party manifesto positions on voters' perceptions of opposition and cabinet parties. These estimates can be found in Table 8, where the headline value is the median estimated effect size with the 95% confidence interval bracketed below. Before considering the hypotheses, the first thing we note is that the recovered persistence value, the proportion of the concurrently observed dependent variable explained by the lagged dependent variable, is almost identical to the panel data benchmark and very efficiently estimated. We believe this similarity indicates that Sophia is a well-calibrated measure and that the model is well specified. As discussed, this level of persistence implies that voters' perceptions of party brands are remarkably stable, but still malleable. Perceptions of party positions *do* change, but, on average, change is not dramatic from one period to the next.

Hypothesis μ_1 predicted that perceptions of coalition parties would be positively influenced by the positions of their partners in government, and the results in Table 8 show that the expected correlation is manifest in the data and quite large. Shifting the focal party's partners in government 1 unit to the right results in an immediate 0.125-unit shift to the right in how that party is perceived, with a theoretical indefinite term effect of 0.631, holding all other factors constant (conditions we are confident will not hold). This result reconfirms a relationship that has been found several times over in previous

Table 8 Short- and long-term effects of party positions and cabinet ideology on voter perceptions

	Government	Opposition
Persistence	0.843	
	[0.820, 0.866]	
Cabinet ideology		
STE x_t	0.125	−0.037
	[0.072, 0.178]	[−0.073, 0.000]
STE x_{t-1}	−0.025	−0.031
	[−0.079, 0.003]	[−0.068, 0.005]
LTE x	0.638	−0.433
	[0.293, 0.988]	[−0.698, −0.179]
Manifesto position		
STE x_t	0.080	0.154
	[−0.015, 0.172]	[0.078, 0.229]
STE x_{t-1}	0.029	0.022
	[−0.064, 0.124]	[−0.047, 0.092]
LTE x	0.695	1.124
	[0.081, 1.283]	[0.775, 1.461]

research. The complementary relationship hypothesized in μ_2 is also manifest, and this finding is novel in the extant literature. Voters' perceptions of opposition parties are negatively reactive to the government's position, as voters seem to pull opposition parties away from the cabinet in the policy space. Here, a 1-unit change in the position of the cabinet results in voter perceptions of opposition parties moving 0.037 units *away* from the cabinet in the short term, with a theoretical indefinite term effect of a 0.434-unit shift away from the cabinet, again, holding all other factors constant.

We note that these findings comport with both of the two central understandings of how the left–right metaphor is used to understand political interactions. The first is a policy-dominant organization of political information, as we employ here. In this frame, voters are receiving *policy* cues from patterns of government formation, inferring similarity and difference in the policy preferences of parties that do and do not coalesce. The second is a more general understanding of broader similarity and difference, inclusive of policy preferences but also non-policy social or cultural connections (e.g., Lipset and Lukkan 1967), wherein, for example, some parties may be seen as "left" because their supporters are more educated or "right" because their supporters tend to live in more rural areas. In this frame, voters are receiving more general compatibility signals and using coalition government formation to understand "who goes with whom" across a larger array of non-policy dimensions.

Hypotheses μ_3 and μ_4 predict that manifesto positions will be positively incorporated into voters' perceptions of all parties, but that the effect will be greater for opposition parties relative to their governing counterparts, as governing parties are more likely to have their policy statements crowded out by their record of governance. The data reflect both expectations, where the difference between voters' responsiveness to the policy statements of government and opposition parties is primarily driven by muted immediate reactions to the policy statements of government parties relative to their counterparts in opposition.

In both cases, however, voters' perceptions are very responsive to platforms over the long term, with the theoretical indefinite term effect being very close to 1 for opposition parties, and about 70% of that information eventually incorporated for governing parties. This is consistent with the crowd-out effect we discussed earlier, where changes to policy preferences are given less attention or weight in the short term but are eventually quite impactful over the long term. We also note that the long-term estimate for government parties is much less efficient than the estimate for opposition parties.[26] We did not hypothesize this efficiency difference but find it sufficiently interesting to note here.

From our perspective, the most important substantive conclusion here is the quite large and durable effect of platform changes for opposition parties and the smaller but still quite large effects for governing parties. These results match our qualitative understanding of party politics – parties expend the majority of their resources communicating their policy goals to voters. Yet recall that the effect of manifesto change on voter perceptions is one of the more unstable estimated correlations in the literature, which is particularly surprising given the strong (and commonsensical) ex ante theoretical case for a positive relationship and the lack of basically any theoretical case for a null relationship. Why is it that the long-term effect we have uncovered here is a more or less perfect match to a priori expectations but previous results have been mixed? We believe it is a function of having more data, a better measurement approach, and an appropriate, flexible model specification.

To test hypotheses $\sigma_1^2 : \sigma_4^2$, we calculate the effect of governing status, manifesto uncertainty, manifesto change, and European elections (relative to national elections) on the conditional variance of voters' perceptions of

---

[26] Indeed, the standard deviation on the long-term effect estimates for government parties is nearly twice as large as it is for opposition parties.

Substantive effects for perception variance

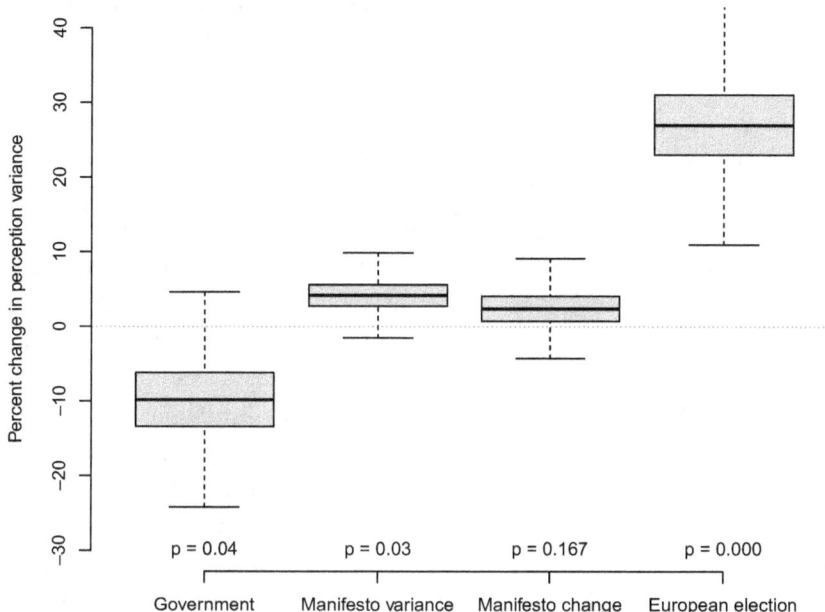

Figure 8 Substantive effects for perception variance.

parties and plot these effects in Figure 8. Regarding Hypothesis σ_1^2, the data suggest that perceptions of cabinet parties are significantly less variable than perceptions of opposition parties. The median estimate here is about a 10% reduction in the conditional variance of perceptions of cabinet parties relative to their opposition counterparts. As discussed, we believe that this difference is driven by the increased availability of information regarding cabinet parties, which leads to a higher level of aggregate certainty over their positions. We should note, however, that of the four correlations we assess in this subsection, this is the most model dependent. Its estimate is more sensitive to dynamic specifications and the inclusion/exclusion of party seat shares, as seat shares are highly correlated with government participation. As such, we encourage our readers to take this particular result with a grain of salt, as more research is needed to find a more stable and accurate estimate of the relationship between governing status, party size, and the variability of voters' perceptions.

No such grain of salt is required for the correlation implied by Hypothesis σ_2^2, however. Parties that issue less certain or higher-variance electoral platforms are viewed with significantly less certainty than parties that issue more certain or lower-variance platforms. A one standard deviation increase in the manifesto position standard error increases the conditional variance of voters' perceptions by about 5%, and we are quite certain of the direction of this relationship. This relationship also exhibits comparatively low levels of model dependence, so we are more confident in our interpretation of the data here. The estimated relationship suggests, intuitively, that clearer policy position signals lead to clearer perceptions of parties' policy brands. The strength of this result in both magnitude and efficiency suggests that parties have substantial capacity to strategically shape aggregate certainty over their policy intentions, which some previous scholarship suggests may redound to their electoral benefit (Somer-Topcu 2015; Lo, Proksch, and Slapin 2016; Lehrer and Lin 2020).

The effects of change in policy commitments from one election to the next are indistinguishable from zero. Recall that Hypothesis σ_3^2 predicted that larger changes in party platforms would increase the variance in voters' perceptions of those parties, but the data do not bear this out. The median estimate is in the expected (positive) direction, but 16% of the posterior distribution of estimates are negative, so we cannot reject the null hypothesis in this case.

We also note, however, that if this particular relationship did indeed exist, observational studies may not be able to uncover it, given the strong incentives parties have to maintain stable brands (e.g., Enelow and Hinich 1984; Budge 1994; Aldrich 1995). Given these incentives, the on-equilibrium behaviors of rational parties may result in a distribution of platform changes that is too small to have any meaningful substantive effect on the variance of voters' perceptions. We know that party platforms *do* change, and the results above show that these changes are perceived by voters; however, it is possible that parties are too savvy to make changes large enough to elicit confusion in the electorate.

Our final estimated relationship is the effect of election type, specifically European parliamentary elections relative to national elections. Hypothesis σ_4^2 predicted that the conditional variance of party perceptions would be greater in the shadow of a European election relative to national elections because voters simply care less about EP contests than those for their national parliament. This may cause a paucity of available information about EP elections – as media may cover EP contests less fervently than national elections – but it would certainly reduce the salience of the available partisan information to voters. The data bear this out. Conditional variance of voter perceptions is over 25% greater about EP elections relative to national elections. This is the most consequential of the hypothesized relationships for σ^2 by far, and it supports previous research suggesting that, to voters, EP elections are "second-order" elections with less at stake than national contests (Franklin and Hobolt 2011; Hobolt and Wittrock 2011; Hobolt and Spoon 2012). Our findings here show that the lack of enthusiasm for participation in EP contests not only depresses turnout but also depresses clarity of understanding of the policies that contestants in the election are offering.

4.4 Discussion

Our goal in this section was to apply our theoretical framework, data, and modeling strategy to holistically study voters' perceptions of parties in the left–right space, considering both the mean and variance of those perceptions. We tested eight hypotheses, half corresponding to the mean position and half corresponding to the variance. Reconfirming past findings, our analysis revealed that perceptions of cabinet parties are positively responsive to the position their partners in coalition. For what we believe is the first time, we found that perceptions of opposition parties are negatively responsive to the position of the government, indicating that the typical voter tends to push cabinet parties together in the metaphorical left–right space, while pulling the opposition away from the government's center of gravity. The data also revealed interesting differences in voters' responsiveness to changes in party platform. While voters seem to positively incorporate manifesto changes for all parties, the positive response is much stronger for opposition parties relative to their counterparts in government, presumably because government parties have their policy *promises* crowded out by their record of producing policy *outcomes*.

In analyzing the variance of voters' perceptions, we found conditional evidence that voters' perceptions of cabinet parties are less variable than their perceptions of opposition parties, strong evidence that clearer policy platforms are correlated with more certain perceptions of policy position, but no evidence that positional changes in platforms exacerbate voters' uncertainty over parties' positions, but there are some caveats to this conclusion, given parties' incentives. Finally, we found quite strong evidence that voters', perceptions exhibit much less variance around national elections than around European parliamentary elections, presumably because European elections are substantially less important to the typical voter. Each of these variance findings is new to the literature.

It is our hope that this exercise not only allows our colleagues to learn something new about how voters generate and update their perceptions of parties policy positions, but also shows the utility of the theoretical framework, data, and modeling strategy that we present here in hopes that they may employ one or more of these tools in their own research. In Section 5 we discuss a number of open questions that may be tackled with these tools.

5 Where to Go from Here

Our goals in writing this Element were to provide a fairly simple, direct definition of voter perceptions of parties' policy positions; present a theoretical framework for generating and scrutinizing falsifiable arguments about what types of events should (re)shape perceptions; and collect and disseminate a large data archive with improved measurement of perceptions, as well as a simple, flexible statistical model in order to test these arguments. In so doing, we also hoped to convince our colleagues that studying voters' party perceptions is a worthwhile (and fun) pursuit. To that end, we want to close out this Element by discussing several avenues for future research – in well-established areas, more nascent strands, and what we feel are promising new directions – that we believe would make excellent articles, dissertations, or book projects.

First, the extant literature on voter perceptions, including this Element, exists in a type of institution-free world in which we focus more or less exclusively on parliamentary systems and assume away (typically implicitly) institutional variation that almost certainly affects party perceptions. Of course, there are a few exceptions here – for example, Carroll and Kubo (2018, 2021) analyze the effect of democratic consolidation and party polarization on the nature of voters' perceptions of parties, and Fortunato, Stevenson, and Vonnahme (2016) argue that voters will collect and retain higher-quality information on parties' locations in settings where that information is more useful for understanding political processes, particularly the formation of coalition cabinets. Those exceptions withstanding, on the institutional front, we are barely scratching the surface. We want to address several basic guiding questions: In what context do parties compete; who composes parties; what do parties do; how are they organized; etc. Where to begin?

We are fascinated by how federalism or supranational governing structures may shape how parties are perceived. Parties in Brazil, Germany, or India face different types of organizational challenges than parties in unitary systems like Korea, the Netherlands, or Uruguay. First, provincial party organizations have strong incentives to vary their positions from the national platform in order to appeal to local voters and maximize vote returns in provincial contests, but this runs the risk of blurring the national brand and potentially costing votes in national elections, or elections in other (perhaps neighboring) provinces. Second, the nature of voters' perceptions of parties' positions at the national level may be impacted by electoral competitiveness or party strategy at the regional level (Fortunato and Stevenson 2021; Spoon and Nonnemacher 2024). Supranational party organizations, particularly those competing for seats in the European Parliament, face similar challenges with their national counterparts.

The relevance to voters' perceptions, of course, is assessing the impact of these parties' strategic decisions. Are provincial deviations from national platforms manifest in voters' perceptions and, if so, what are the relative weights of provincial and national platforms in voters' perceptions? Does the formation of coalition governments at the provincial level have similar effects on voters' perceptions of parties as the formation of federal-level governments? Are perceptions of party positions simply more variable in federalist contexts – or contexts in which supranational organizations also compete – than their unitary counterparts, all else equal? Scholars may find that the entrance of countries into the European Union (EU) and changes in the distribution of policy authority between central and provincial governments (for example the 2001 Italian constitutional amendment) may offer opportunities to gain traction on these questions.

Focusing on parliamentary systems at the national level, we think electoral institutions should have pronounced effects on voters' incentives and ability to collect information on party positions. More permissive institutions lead to more viable parties, which should influence voters' ability to find a good match to their ideal policy preferences in the marketplace and may make for more complex party systems that are more difficult for voters to monitor. These rules also influence the extent to which individual candidates are incentivized to cultivate a personal brand apart from the brand established by their parties, which may also complicate the competition space. A recent book by Crisp et al. (2025) studies and measures these electoral system properties, which they shorthand as interparty and intraparty competition. Marrying the arguments, insights, and measures from that book with our work here could yield several fascinating contributions on the institutional determinants of voters' party perceptions. Do more permissive electoral institutions degrade the responsiveness of voter perceptions to platform change by increasing the competition space and allowing the proliferation of parties (increasing the relative cost of collecting and maintaining platform information)? Do institutions that incentivize the cultivation of individual candidate brands generate competing candidate and party signals that increase the variance of voters' party perceptions?

Related to candidates' incentives for individual brand cultivation is the diversity of candidates or distribution of membership across relevant groups. There is evidence that women party leaders are correlated with more moderate perceptions of party preferences (O'Brien 2019), and also that having more women in a party's parliamentary delegation leads voters to believe that the party is more left on average (Adams et al. 2024). This should be only the beginning. The distribution of women within a party delegation or a party writ large is likely to have substantial effects on both a party's actual policy positions as well as voters' perceptions of those positions across more or less all jurisdictions. Of course, there are many different observable characteristics of comprising membership diversity to study. We may consider the distribution of age, class, occupation, religion, or many other potentially relevant (or irrelevant) observable characteristics for voters' perceptions of parties. Whether these characteristics are actually observable and informative to parties' positions may inform one set of questions, and whether voters *infer* that they are informative, potentially due to the application of associated stereotypes (e.g., O'Brien 2019), may inform another.

In keeping with a broader theme of the Element, there is a great deal of promise in considering new (or reconsidering existing) avenues for parties to communicate their policy positions to voters, both *about* and *between* elections – considering what parties *do* in addition to what parties *say*. There is some existing research on parties' non-manifesto strategies for communicating with their supporters. They can issue press releases or direct communications (Sagarzazu and Klüver 2017) or engage in prime minister debates (Sagarzazu and Williams 2017), change their media strategies (Somer-Topcu, Tavits, and Baumann 2020), use their plenary speech time (Martin and Vanberg 2008), or submit legislative amendments (Fortunato 2019b) in order to signal to potential voters what policies they do and do not support. Research on these types of communication strategies is just getting off the ground, with the possible exception of research on the informational roles of leadership changes, where researchers have found that leadership turnover increases voters' responsiveness to platform changes (Fernandez-Vazquez and Somer-Topcu 2019) and decreases the variance of those responses (Somer-Topcu 2017).

Apart from leadership research, how parties employ non-manifesto venues to signal their policy positions and whether or not voters are responsive to these signals are essentially open questions, but not questions lacking guidance in the extant research. Fortunato (2021, p. 27) provides a detailed discussion of how collective responsibility constrains the signaling strategies of cabinet participants, as well as a kind of institutional mapping for which parliamentary processes may or may not provide a reasonable venue for disseminating such signals and how such signals may be issued in parliamentary procedure:

> It is heated debate in the plenary, pointed questions of ministers in subpoenaed testimony in committee hearings, and bold amendments in legislative review. Wherever the process allows for confrontation and conflict, we should observe it, provided that three conditions are met. The procedures must be sufficiently (a) open, (b) salient, and (c) individualized to meaningfully shape media narrative in order to observe differentiating conflict and, the degree to which these criteria are met can and should vary cross-nationally according to institutional structures.

Though Fortunato's focus was specifically on cabinet partners, the institutional characteristics extend to all parties. Do procedures like legislative review and scrutiny allow for parties to create individualized (party-level) records of policy influence?[27] Are committee meetings open and recorded? Are plenary debates unconstrained, or dominated by the cabinet? These institutional parameters can and should be leveraged to discover contextual variations in both the selection and effectiveness of parties' communicative strategies. That institutional perspective, combined with early empirical findings by Fortunato (2021), Somer-Topcu and Tavits (2023), and Santoso, Stevenson, and Weschle (2024) showing that voters seem to be responsive to direct and media-moderated partisan signals from a variety of fora, provide theoretical and empirical guidance to jump-start investigation into these questions. We believe that research here, studying the intersection of voters' perceptions and parties' strategies, will be critical to comparative politics and our understanding of democratic processes around the world. There is substantial opportunity for impact by aspiring (or established) scholars on these questions.

Many of these open questions are quite general. How do parties choose signaling venues to message voters? What type of party actions bear the most weight in reshaping voters' perceptions? Particularly important here, we believe, is research on parties' effort allocation. Does the electoral imperative to send policy signals in a variety of fora crowd out real policymaking effort; or, what do parties do when faced with tough choices over maximizing social welfare by supporting a policy that is discordant with their previous commitments or protecting their brand in the eyes of voters? These are difficult questions to answer, but we believe that scholars will find pursuing the answers not just challenging, but interesting and fun.

Stepping back from parties' incentives to use parliamentary procedure to communicate with voters, there are also questions of how core policymaking institutions affect the manner in which parties are perceived, particularly parties in government, but also in opposition. That is, fundamental differences in policymaking institutions shape the distribution of policy influence across coalition partners. Some systems endow prime ministers with substantial power to exert leverage on their partners in government or opposition. Among these powers is likely the ability to unilaterally call elections, but the power to recall bills from committee or force them onto the agenda against the wishes of other actors is also important. These may shape, for example, the extent to which prime ministerial parties draw voters' perceptions of their junior partners into their orbit by creating a sustained media message of the prime ministerial party winning policy disagreements, or just getting what it wants at nearly every turn.

---

[27] For example, Norway's committee reports attribute proposed and accepted amendments to "the majority" and rejected amendments to "the minority," whereas Belgium's reports log the individual sponsors.

Relatedly, parliaments vary in their capacity to win policy disagreements with proposing ministers and therefore their capacity to enforce the terms of coalition bargains (Martin and Vanberg 2011, 2014). It is only natural that these differences drive variability in the extent to which cabinet participation (or nonparticipation) reshapes voters' perceptions.

Of course, the policy outcomes themselves are important and have only recently begun to be studied. Adams, Bernardi, and Wlezien (2020) find some evidence that voters seem attuned to key policy choices made by governments, in this case, welfare spending, updating their perceptions of governing parties' policy positions as more right when they decrease welfare spending. A previous, related study tracks the responsiveness of voters' government support vis-à-vis welfare spending output and welfare rhetoric, finding greater responsiveness to outcomes than promises (Bernardi and Adams 2019) and relating this finding to the "thermostatic" model of public opinion (Soroka and Wlezien 2010). We believe that more research on this question is warranted, not only for normative reasons – voters *should* be responsive to government actions if they are to hold government parties responsible for their actions – but also because they present interesting theoretical and empirical problems to solve.

How do specific policy jurisdictions and policy outputs map on to our CCS framework? To which policies are voters attuned, and does the set of policies voters are attuned to vary over space and time? Are responses direct, or do voters only respond in light of the policy choices becoming fodder for political debate in media or between parties? Based on our previous arguments, we suspect issues that are more immediate or tangible bear greater weight than issues that are distant or abstract. For instance, we would expect greater responsiveness to welfare spending and personal taxation than to foreign aid spending or bespoke regulatory policy pertaining to a small industry. Of course, voters' ability to correctly place parties on specific issue positions likely relies on the salience of those issues (Somer-Topcu, Fournier, and Dassonneville 2025). Applied research is needed here, and opportunity abounds.

Staying within parliamentary systems, we believe that one of the greatest opportunities for new research revolves around the organization and development of party systems. Following the dissolution of the Soviet Union, several former Soviet republics transitioned to democratic, parliamentary governance (with fairly permissive party systems). This process demanded unusually fast (relative to consolidated democracies) formation of new political parties, which creates an interesting and novel challenge for new voters who have not been politically socialized under democracy with existing parties. There is excellent research on the transition and its impact on voters by many scholars (e.g., Pacek 1994; Bohrer, Pacek, and Radcliff 2000; Duch 2001; Tucker 2006), and

Tavits in particular (e.g., 2005, 2008, 2013), but there is still ample opportunity for investigation on the development of parties as manifest in voters' perceptions.

Recall from Section 4 that a party's age was a significant negative predictor of variance in voters' perceptions of its position. Countries with a recent transition to democracy provide an unusual opportunity to trace the consolidation of party positions in the mass public while their development is still nascent in a way that we could not in the case of, say, Denmark or the Netherlands, which democratized well in advance of modern survey methods. One may compare, for example, perceptions of German parties across the former East and West German states to track how long it takes adults to form fairly consistent, durable perceptions of parties when they are socialized into young adulthood with and without their presence. One may also compare the republics that formerly composed Yugoslavia to track how differing electoral or parliamentary institutions condition the development of consistent party brand perceptions among voters of similar pre-democratic socialization. Indeed, similar, though potentially not quite as clean, opportunities are also present in the recent transitions back to democracy in Greece, Portugal, and Spain (it can be easy to forget how recently many European countries were nondemocratic). Research of this nature would not only help us better understand our past but also put us in a position to make more reasonable and accurate predictions about the nature of (hopefully many) future transitions to democratic governance.

All of this discussion has been focused on parliamentary democracies, which, of course, omits much of Africa and most of the Western Hemisphere. How does a directly elected chief executive – in concurrent or nonconcurrent legislative elections – influence the extent to which parties are able to cultivate stable policy positions? Which campaigns take precedence, or bear the most weight in voters' party perceptions? How does the formation of legislative coalitions and potentially differing executive coalitions influence voters' perceptions of similarities and differences among parties' positions? How do electoral incentives toward personalism more generally (Crisp et al. 2025) affect the manner in which parties attempt to cultivate durable brands and their ability to do so? The central role of the president in coalition formation and operation, combined with the higher complexity of party systems in presidential multiparty democracies – characterized by higher fragmentation and less institutionalized and nationalized political parties – makes gathering data on party positions and studying voter perceptions more challenging but also opens up a completely new area to explore. There are already fascinating studies available (e.g., Dahlberg 2013; Lupu 2013, 2016; Carroll and Kubo 2018; Junqueira, Silva, and Whitten 2025), but there is room for much more research and there are substantial opportunities for analyzing voter perceptions while incorporating differences in systems of government, electoral systems, and policymaking institutions.

What all of these suggestions have in common is a focus on voter perceptions as the outcome, but, as we mentioned in Section 1, these perceptions are a key factor in vote choice. As such, policy perceptions are likely to animate partisan decision-making in more or less all observable fora. At the time of writing, however, only Fortunato (2019b, 2021) has modeled voter perceptions directly as a predictor of legislative behavior in these systems, arguing that parties make legislative choices to influence the manner in which they are perceived by voters. This is in part due to the lack of availability of data on how voters perceive parties. We draw this conclusion because there is a fairly large amount of research pointing to control of party positions as a central incentive for party behaviors inside and outside legislatures. For instance, Martin and Vanberg (2008) argue that parties use their parliamentary speeches to clarify their positions on issues upon which coalition participation may have muddied their brand and use alternative measures of party positions as a proxy for perceived brands. Sagarzazu and Klüver (2017) make a similar argument and leverage differing time points in the electoral cycle to isolate their mechanism. There are several interesting, recent contributions making related arguments and using related designs. We recommend Whitaker and Martin (2022), Nonnemacher and Spoon (2023), and Poljak and Walter (2023) to begin.

We contend that voters' perceptions should be a pervasive influence on parties' choices, particularly in outward-facing interactions – party actions that are open, salient, and individualized (Fortunato 2021). Legislative proposals, legislative review and scrutiny, parliamentary speeches, direct messaging such as press releases and social media posts, and, of course, party platforms are all strategic choices made with an eye toward affecting how the party is perceived by potential supporters. These choices, made both by parties as individual actors and in response to one another, are made throughout the entire inter-electoral period, but only recently have we begun to study them in earnest (see, e.g., Martin and Vanberg 2005, 2011; Fortunato 2021, for more discussion here). There is a clear need for more research on these ongoing processes and how electoral (brand maintenance) incentives shape them.

For instance, Meyer and Wagner (2019, 2023) argue that parties strategically allocate effort to communicating their positions on different issues to shape voters' overall perceptions of their brand – emphasizing issues on which they are more left if there is an electoral incentive to appear more left-leaning to the electorate. This strategy allows parties to send differing but still credible signals of policy intention without going back on previous policy commitments.

What would the deployment of this strategy look like when parties are making hard choices over their approach to governance? Cabinet parties control multiple ministerial portfolios and have agency over the allocation of their proposal opportunities across those portfolios. It seems reasonable that they would prioritize issues on which their preferences are better aligned with where they want voters to perceive their overall position. With very few exceptions (e.g., Martin 2004; König et al. 2022), however, these choices have not been studied, leaving plenty of room for enterprising researchers to set the agenda on this research moving forward.

Likewise, parties' choices over how they spend their finite resources in parliamentary debate or ministers' questions are similarly understudied. We have gathered substantial data archives of legislative speeches (e.g., Sylvester, Greene, and Ebing 2022) with a level of detail that permits extraordinarily ambitious research designs. A recent review of the literature by Fernandes, Debus, and Bäck (2021) makes clear that there is substantial opportunity here, particularly to extend or generalize the theoretical arguments of Proksch and Slapin (2012, 2015), shifting focus toward interpartisan politics and the brand incentives at play there. For instance, while Proksch and Slapin (2012, 2015) are centrally concerned with whom parties allow to speak for them, new research may reorient toward to whom parties are speaking in response. Do the political incentives for differentiation Fortunato (2021) documented in legislative scrutiny and amending also play out in parliamentary speeches? Do they play out equivalently across policy jurisdictions, or do parties prioritize certain issues strategically as Meyer and Wagner (2019, 2023) would predict? Perhaps these choices are even telegraphed at the formation of governments when parties bargain over not just the allocation of ministries (Bäck, Debus, and Dumont 2011; Martin and Vanberg 2020), but their responsibilities (Sieberer et al. 2021; Klüser 2024), adjoining junior ministers (Thies 2001; Lipsmeyer and Pierce 2011), and opposing committee chairs (Carroll and Cox 2012; Fortunato, Martin, and Vanberg 2019).

Each of these interesting, open questions lends itself to at least one of the three contributions we set out to make in this Element, and we hope that we have convinced our readers that these open questions would be exhilarating to answer as well as worth answering. This is an exciting and important subfield of comparative politics, but one that is still young and relatively limited in both the scope of questions and accumulated knowledge. There is much to learn, and we hope that you will contribute to this growing field and find our contributions in this Element helpful tools in pushing the field forward.

References

Achen, Christopher H. 1992. "Social psychology, demographic variables, and linear regression: Breaking the iron triangle in voting research." *Political Behavior* 14:195–211.

Adams, James. 2001. "A theory of spatial competition with biased voters: Party policies viewed temporally and comparatively." *British Journal of Political Science* 31(1):121–158.

Adams, James, Luca Bernardi, and Christopher Wlezien. 2020. "Social welfare policy outputs and governing parties' left–right images: Do voters respond?" *Journal of Politics* 82(3):1161–1165.

Adams, James, David Bracken, Noam Gidron, Will Horne, Seonghui Lee, Diana Z. O'Brien, Philip Santoso, Kaitlin Senk, and Randolph T. Stevenson. 2024. "Gender inclusivity shifts parties' images leftward: Observational and experimental evidence." Unpublished manuscript, University of Essex.

Adams, James, Michael Clark, Lawrence Ezrow, and Garrett Glasgow. 2006. "Are niche parties fundamentally different from mainstream parties? The causes and the electoral consequences of Western European parties' policy shifts, 1976–1998." *American Journal of Political Science* 50(3):513–529.

Adams, James, Catherine E. De Vries, and Debra Leiter. 2012. "Subconstituency reactions to elite depolarization in the Netherlands: An analysis of the Dutch public's policy beliefs and partisan loyalties, 1986–98." *British Journal of Political Science* 42(1):81–105.

Adams, James, Lawrence Ezrow, and Christopher Wlezien. 2016. "The company you keep: How voters infer party positions on European integration from governing coalition arrangements." *American Journal of Political Science* 60(4):811–823.

Adams, James, Lawrence Ezrow, and Zeynep Somer-Topcu. 2011. "Is anybody listening? Evidence that voters do not respond to European parties' policy statements during elections." *American Journal of Political Science* 55(2):370–382.

Adams, James, Lawrence Ezrow, and Zeynep Somer-Topcu. 2014. "Do voters respond to party manifestos or to a wider information environment? An analysis of mass-elite linkages on European integration." *American Journal of Political Science* 58(4):967–978.

Adams, James and Samuel Merril III. 1999. "Modeling party strategies and policy representation in multiparty elections: Why are strategies so extreme?" *American Journal of Political Science* 43(3):765–791.

Adams, James, Simon Weschle, and Christopher Wlezien. 2021. "Elite interactions and voters' perceptions of parties' policy positions." *American Journal of Political Science* 65(1):101–114.

Adams, James and Zeynep Somer-Topcu. 2009. "Moderate now, win votes later: The electoral consequences of parties' policy shifts in 25 postwar democracies." *Journal of Politics* 71(2):678–692.

Aldrich, John H. 1995. *Why Parties? The Origin and Transformation of Political Parties in America.* Chicago, IL: University of Chicago Press.

Alvarez, R. Michael and John Brehm. 1995. "American ambivalence towards abortion policy: Development of a heteroskedastic probit model of competing values." *American Journal of Political Science* 39(4):1055–1082.

Alvarez, R. Michael and Charles H. Franklin. 1994. "Uncertainty and political perceptions." *Journal of Politics* 56(3):671–688.

Bäck, Hanna, Markus Baumann, Marc Debus, and Jochen Müller. 2019. "The unequal distribution of speaking time in parliamentary-party groups." *Legislative Studies Quarterly* 44(1):163–193.

Bäck, Hanna, Marc Debus, and Patrick Dumont. 2011. "Who gets what in coalition governments? Predictors of portfolio allocation in parliamentary democracies." *European Journal of Political Research* 50(4):441–478.

Banducci, Susan, Heiko Giebler, and Sylvia Kritzinger. 2017. "Knowing more from less: How the information environment increases knowledge of party positions." *British Journal of Political Science* 47(3):571–588.

Bartels, Larry M. 1986. "Issue voting under uncertainty: An empirical test." *American Journal of Political Science* 30(4):709–728.

Bartels, Larry M. 2002. "Beyond the running tally: Partisan bias in political perceptions." *Political Behavior* 24:117–150.

Baumgartner, Frank R. and Laura Chaqués Bonafont. 2015. "All news is bad news: Newspaper coverage of political parties in Spain." *Political Communication* 32(2):268–291.

Bawn, Kathleen and Zeynep Somer-Topcu. 2012. "Government versus opposition at the polls: How governing status affects the impact of policy positions." *American Journal of Political Science* 56(2):433–446.

Benoit, Kenneth, Michael Laver, and Slava Mikhaylov. 2009. "Treating words as data with error: Uncertainty in text statements of policy positions." *American Journal of Political Science* 53(2):495–513.

Bernardi, Luca and James Adams. 2019. "Does government support respond to governments' social welfare rhetoric or their spending? An analysis of government support in Britain, Spain and the United States." *British Journal of Political Science* 49(4):1407–1429.

Bohrer II, Robert E., Alexander C. Pacek, and Benjamin Radcliff. 2000. "Electoral participation, ideology, and party politics in post-communist Europe." *Journal of Politics* 62(4):1161–1172.

Budge, Ian. 1994. "A new spatial theory of party competition: Uncertainty, ideology and policy equilibria viewed comparatively and temporally." *British Journal of Political Science* 24(4):443–467.

Carroll, Royce and Gary W. Cox. 2012. "Shadowing ministers: Monitoring partners in coalition governments." *Comparative Political Studies* 45(2):220–236.

Carroll, Royce and Hiroki Kubo. 2018. "Explaining citizen perceptions of party ideological positions: The mediating role of political contexts." *Electoral Studies* 51:14–23.

Carroll, Royce and Hiroki Kubo. 2021. "Measuring and explaining the complexity of left–right perceptions of political parties." *Electoral Studies* 71:102310.

Cox, Gary W. 1997. *Making Votes Count*. Cambridge: Cambridge University Press.

Cox, Gary W. 1987. *The Efficient Secret: The Cabinet and the Development of Political Parties in Victorian England*. Cambridge: Cambridge University Press.

Cox, Gary W. 1990. "Centripetal and centrifugal incentives in electoral systems." *American Journal of Political Science* 34(4):903–935.

Cox, Gary W. and Mathew D. McCubbins. 2005. *Setting the Agenda: Responsible Party Government in the US House of Representatives*. Cambridge: Cambridge University Press.

Crisp, Brian F., Patrick Cunha Silva, Santiago, Olivella, and Guillermo Rosas. 2025. *Electoral System Incentives for Interparty and Intraparty Politics*. Oxford: Oxford University Press.

Dahlberg, Stefan. 2013. "Does context matter: The impact of electoral systems, political parties and individual characteristics on voters' perceptions of party positions." *Electoral Studies* 32(4):670–683.

Dalton, Russell J. 2014. *Citizen Politics: Public Opinion and Political Parties in Advanced Industrial Democracies*. Washington, DC: CQ Press.

Dalton, Russell J. and Ian McAllister. 2015. "Random walk or planned excursion? Continuity and change in the left–right positions of political parties." *Comparative Political Studies* 48(6):759–787.

De Boef, Suzanna and Luke Keele. 2008. "Taking time seriously." *American Journal of Political Science* 52(1):184–200.

De Vreese, Claes H., Susan A. Banducci, Holli A. Semetko, and Hajo G. Boomgaarden. 2006. "The news coverage of the 2004 European Parliamentary election campaign in 25 countries." *European Union Politics* 7(4):477–504.

Duch, Raymond M. 2001. "A developmental model of heterogeneous economic voting in new democracies." *American Political Science Review* 95(4):895–910.

Duch, Raymond M., Jeff May, and David A. Armstrong. 2010. "Coalition-directed voting in multiparty democracies." *American Political Science Review* 104(4):698–719.

Duch, Raymond M. and Randolph T. Stevenson. 2008. *The Economic Vote: How Political and Economic Institutions Condition Election Results.* Cambridge: Cambridge University Press.

Enelow, James M. and Melvin J. Hinich. 1984. *The Spatial Theory of Voting: An Introduction.* Cambridge: Cambridge University Press.

Erikson, Robert S., Michael B. MacKuen, and James A. Stimson. 2002. *The Macro Polity.* Cambridge: Cambridge University Press.

Ezrow, Lawrence. 2007. "The variance matters: How party systems represent the preferences of voters." *Journal of Politics* 69(1):182–192.

Ezrow, Lawrence, Jonathan Homola, and Margit Tavits. 2014. "When extremism pays: Policy positions, voter certainty, and party support in postcommunist Europe." *Journal of Politics* 76(2):535–547.

Ezrow, Lawrence, Margit Tavits, and Jonathan Homola. 2014. "Voter polarization, strength of partisanship, and support for extremist parties." *Comparative Political Studies* 47(11):1558–1583.

Falcó-Gimeno, Albert and Pablo Fernandez-Vazquez. 2020. "Choices that matter: Coalition formation and parties' ideological reputations." *Political Science Research and Methods* 8(2):285–300.

Fearon, James D. 1995. "Rationalist explanations for war." *International Organization* 49(3):379–414.

Fernandes, Jorge M., Marc Debus, and Hanna Bäck. 2021. "Unpacking the politics of legislative debates." *European Journal of Political Research* 60(4):1032–1045.

Fernandez-Vazquez, Pablo. 2014. "And yet it moves: The effect of election platforms on party policy images." *Comparative Political Studies* 47(14):1919–1944.

Fernandez-Vazquez, Pablo. 2018. "Voter discounting of party campaign manifestos: An analysis of mainstream and niche parties in Western Europe, 1971–2011." *Party Politics* 26(4):471–483.

Fernandez-Vazquez, Pablo. 2019. "The credibility of party policy rhetoric survey experimental evidence." *Journal of Politics* 81(1):309–314.

Fernandez-Vazquez, Pablo and Zeynep Somer-Topcu. 2019. "The informational role of party leader changes on voter perceptions of party positions." *British Journal of Political Science* 49(3):977–996.

Fiorina, Morris P. 1981. *Retrospective Voting in American National Elections*. New Haven, CT: Yale University Press.

Fortunato, David. 2019a. "The electoral implications of coalition policy making." *British Journal of Political Science* 49:59–80.

Fortunato, David. 2019b. "Legislative review and party differentiation in coalition governments." *American Political Science Review* 113(1):242–247.

Fortunato, David. 2021. *The Cycle of Coalition: How Parties and Voters Interact under Coalition Governance*. Cambridge: Cambridge University Press.

Fortunato, David, Lanny W. Martin, and Georg Vanberg. 2019. "Committee chairs and legislative review in parliamentary democracies." *British Journal of Political Science* 49(2):785–797.

Fortunato, David and Randolph T. Stevenson. 2013a. "Perceptions of partisan ideologies: The effect of coalition participation." *American Journal of Political Science* 57(2):459–477.

Fortunato, David and Randolph T. Stevenson. 2013b. "Performance voting and knowledge of cabinet composition." *Electoral Studies* 32(3):517–523.

Fortunato, David and Randolph T. Stevenson. 2021. "Party government and political information." *Legislative Studies Quarterly* 46(2):251–295.

Fortunato, David, Thiago N. Silva, Rylie Wieseler, and Laron K. Williams. 2024. "Missingness and inferential errors in the study of voters' perceptions of parties' positions." Working Paper, University of Missouri.

Fortunato, David, Randolph T. Stevenson, and Greg Vonnahme. 2016. "Context and political knowledge: Explaining cross-national variation in partisan left–right knowledge." *Journal of Politics* 78(4):1211–1228.

Frankel, Laura Lazarus and D. Sunshine Hillygus. 2014. "Looking beyond demographics: Panel attrition in the ANES and GSS." *Political Analysis* 22(3):336–353.

Franklin, Mark N. and Sara B. Hobolt. 2011. "The legacy of lethargy: How elections to the European Parliament depress turnout." *Electoral Studies* 30(1):67–76.

Gschwend, Thomas. 2001. *Strategic Voting in Mixed Electoral Systems*. New York: State University of New York at Stony Brook Press.

Hjermitslev, Ida B. 2022. "Mainstream sell-outs? How collaboration with the radical right changes perceptions of party positions on immigration." *Government and Opposition* 57(1):31–55.

Hjermitslev, Ida B. 2023. "Collaboration or competition? Experimental evidence for coalition heuristics." *European Journal of Political Research* 62(1):326–337.

Hobolt, Sara B. and Jae-Jae Spoon. 2012. "Motivating the European voter: Parties, issues and campaigns in European Parliament elections." *European Journal of Political Research* 51(6):701–727.

Hobolt, Sara Binzer and Jill Wittrock. 2011. "The second-order election model revisited: An experimental test of vote choices in European Parliament elections." *Electoral Studies* 30(1):29–40.

Honaker, James, Gary King, Matthew Blackwell, et al. 2011. "Amelia II: A program for missing data." *Journal of Statistical Software* 45(7):1–47.

Huddy, Leonie, Lilliana Mason, and Lene Aarøe. 2015. "Expressive partisanship: Campaign involvement, political emotion, and partisan identity." *American Political Science Review* 109(1):1–17.

Junqueira, Andrea, Thiago N. Silva, and Guy D. Whitten. 2025. "Coalition as a heuristic: Voters' perceptions of party positions in presidential multiparty democracies." *Journal of Elections, Public Opinion and Parties*. FirstView.

Kedar, Orit. 2005. "When moderate voters prefer extreme parties: Policy balancing in parliamentary elections." *American Political Science Review* 99(2):185–199.

King, Gary. 1989. *Unifying Political Methodology: The Likelihood Theory of Statistical Inference*. Cambridge: Cambridge University Press.

King, Gary, James Honaker, Anne Joseph, and Kenneth Scheve. 2001. "Analyzing incomplete political science data: An alternative algorithm for multiple imputation." *American Political Science Review* 95(1):49–69.

King, Gary, Michael Tomz and Jason Wittenberg. 2000. "Making the most of statistical analyses: Improving interpretation and presentation." *American Journal of Political Science* 44(2):347–361.

Klüser, K. Jonathan. 2024. "Keeping tabs through collaboration? Sharing ministerial responsibility in coalition governments." *Political Science Research and Methods* 12(1):27–44.

Klüver, Heike and Jae-Jae Spoon. 2016. "Who responds? Voters, parties and issue attention." *British Journal of Political Science* 46(3):633–654.

Klüver, Heike and Jae-Jae Spoon. 2020. "Helping or hurting? How governing as a junior coalition partner influences electoral outcomes." *Journal of Politics* 82(4):1231–1242.

König, Thomas, Nick Lin, Xiao Lu, Thiago N. Silva, Nikoleta Yordanova, and Galina Zudenkova. 2022. "Agenda control and timing of bill initiation: A temporal perspective on coalition governance in parliamentary democracies." *American Political Science Review* 116(1): 231–248.

Laver, Michael. 2005. "Policy and the dynamics of political competition." *American Political Science Review* 99(02):263–281.

Lax, Jeffrey R. and Justin H. Phillips. 2009. "How should we estimate public opinion in the states?" *American Journal of Political Science* 53(1):107–121.

Lehrer, Roni and Nick Lin. 2020. "Everything to everyone? Not when you are internally divided." *Party Politics* 26(6):783–794.

Leischnig, Alexander and Margit Enke. 2011. "Brand stability as a signaling phenomenon: An empirical investigation in industrial markets." *Industrial Marketing Management* 40(7):1116–1122.

Lewis, Jeffrey B. and Drew A. Linzer. 2005. "Estimating regression models in which the dependent variable is based on estimates." *Political Analysis* 13(4):345–364.

Lindstädt, Rene, Sven-Oliver Proksch, and Jonathan B. Slapin. 2016. "When experts disagree: Response aggregation and its consequences in expert surveys." Manuscript, University of Essex, Essex.

Lipset, Seymour Martin and Stein Rokkan. 1967. "Cleavage structures, party systems and voter alignments." In *Party Systems and Voter Alignments: Cross-National Perspectives*, edited by Seymour Martin Lipset and Stein Rokkan. New York: Free Press, pp. 1–64.

Lipsmeyer, Christine S. and Heather Nicole Pierce. 2011. "The eyes that bind: Junior ministers as oversight mechanisms in coalition governments." *Journal of Politics* 73(4):1152–1164.

Little, Andrew T. and Thomas Zeitzoff. 2017. "A bargaining theory of conflict with evolutionary preferences." *International Organization* 71(3): 523–557.

Lo, James, Sven-Oliver Proksch, and Jonathan B. Slapin. 2016. "Ideological clarity in multiparty competition: A new measure and test using election manifestos." *British Journal of Political Science* 46(3):591–610.

Lowe, Will, Kenneth Benoit, Slava Mikhaylov, and Michael Laver. 2011. "Scaling policy preferences from coded political texts." *Legislative Studies Quarterly* 36(1):123–155.

Lupu, Noam. 2013. "Party brands and partisanship: Theory with evidence from a survey experiment in Argentina." *American Journal of Political Science* 57(1):49–64.

Lupu, Noam. 2016. *Party Brands in Crisis: Partisanship, Brand Dilution, and the Breakdown of Political Parties in Latin America*. Cambridge: Cambridge University Press.

Martin, Lanny W. 2004. "The government agenda in parliamentary democracies." *American Journal of Political Science* 48(3):445–461.
URL: *http://www.jstor.org/stable/1519909*

Martin, Lanny W. and Georg Vanberg. 2005. "Coalition policymaking and legislative review." *American Political Science Review* 99:93–106.

Martin, Lanny W. and Georg Vanberg. 2008. "Coalition government and political communication." *Political Research Quarterly* 61:502–516.

Martin, Lanny W. and Georg Vanberg. 2011. *Parliaments and Coalitions: The Role of Legislative Institutions in Multiparty Governance*. Oxford: Oxford University Press.

Martin, Lanny W. and Georg Vanberg. 2014. "Parties and policymaking in multiparty governments: The legislative median, ministerial autonomy, and the coalition compromise." *American Journal of Political Science* 58(4):979–996.

Martin, Lanny W. and Georg Vanberg. 2020. "What you see is not always what you get: Bargaining before an audience under multiparty government." *American Political Science Review* 114(4):1138–1154.

Meguid, Bonnie M. 2005. "Competition between unequals: The role of mainstream party strategy in niche party success." *American Political Science Review* 99(3):347–359.

Meyer, Thomas M. and Markus Wagner. 2019. "It sounds like they are moving: Understanding and modeling emphasis-based policy change." *Political Science Research and Methods* 7(4):757–774.

Nonnemacher, Jeffrey and Jae-Jae Spoon. 2023. "Overcoming the cost of governance? Junior party strategy in multi-level politics." *Party Politics*. 31(1):29–39.

O'Brien, Diana Z. 2019. "Female leaders and citizens' perceptions of political parties." *Journal of Elections, Public Opinion and Parties* 29(4): 465–489.

Pacek, Alexander C. 1994. "Macroeconomic conditions and electoral politics in East Central Europe." *American Journal of Political Science* 38(3): 723–744.

Plescia, Carolina. 2022. "Voters' short-term responsiveness to coalition deals." *Party Politics* 28(5):927–938.

Plescia, Carolina and Magdalena Staniek. 2017. "In the eye of the beholder: Voters' perceptions of party policy shifts." *West European Politics* 40(6):1288–1309.

Poljak, Željko and Annemarie S. Walter. 2023. "Parties' parliamentary attack behaviour throughout the electoral cycle." *Party Politics* 30(5):920–933.

Powell, G. Bingham. 2000. *Elections as Instruments of Democracy: Majoritarian and Proportional Views*. New Haven, CT: Yale University Press.

Powell, Lynda W. 1989. "Analyzing misinformation: Perceptions of congressional candidates' ideologies." *American Journal of Political Science* 33(1):272–293.

Powell, Robert. 2006. "War as a commitment problem." *International Organization* 60(1):169–203.

Proksch, Sven-Oliver and Jonathan B. Slapin. 2012. "Institutional foundations of legislative speech." *American Journal of Political Science* 56(3): 520–537.

Proksch, Sven-Oliver and Jonathan B. Slapin. 2015. *The Politics of Parliamentary Debate*. Cambridge: Cambridge University Press.

Provins, Tessa, Nathan W. Monroe, and David Fortunato. 2022. "Allocating costly influence in legislatures." *Journal of Politics* 84(3):1697–1713.

Reif, Karlheinz and Hermann Schmitt. 1980. "Nine second-order national elections: A conceptual framework for the analysis of European Election results." *European Journal of Political Research* 8(1):3–44.

Sagarzazu, Iñaki and Heike Klüver. 2017. "Coalition governments and party competition: Political communication strategies of coalition parties." *Political Science Research and Methods* 5(2):333–349.

Sagarzazu, Iñaki and Laron K. Williams. 2017. "Making and breaking party leaders? An informational theory of temporary and lasting impacts of prime minister debates in Spain." *Social Science Quarterly* 98(3): 856–875.

Santoso, Lie Philip, Randolph T. Stevenson and Simon Weschle. 2024. "What drives perceptions of partisan cooperation?" *Political Science Research and Methods* 12(4):888–896.

Scarrow, Susan E., Paul D. Webb, and Thomas Poguntke. 2017. *Organizing Political parties: Representation, Participation, and Power*. Oxford: Oxford University Press.

Schelling, Thomas C. 1960. *The Strategy of Conflict: With a New Preface by the Author*. Cambridge, MA: Harvard University Press.

Schumacher, Gijs, Catherine E. De Vries and Barbara Vis. 2013. "Why do parties change position? Party organization and environmental incentives." *Journal of Politics* 75(2):464–477.

Seeberg, Henrik Bech, Rune Slothuus, and Rune Stubager. 2017. "Do voters learn? Evidence that voters respond accurately to changes in political parties' policy positions." *West European Politics* 40(2):336–356.

Shin, Victor and Laron K. Williams. 2024. "The space between: How ideological similarity limits the effectiveness of ambiguity." *Journal of Elections, Public Opinion and Parties*. FirstView.

Sieberer, Ulrich, Thomas M. Meyer, Hanna Bäck et al. 2021. "The political dynamics of portfolio design in European democracies." *British Journal of Political Science* 51(2):772–787.

Silva, Thiago N. 2023. "When do different systems of government lead to similar power-sharing? The case of government formation." *Political Science Research and Methods* 11(4):938–946.

Slantchev, Branislav L. 2003. "The principle of convergence in wartime negotiations." *American Political Science Review* 97(4):621–632.

Söderlund, Peter, Hanna Wass, and André Blais. 2011. "The impact of motivational and contextual factors on turnout in first-and second-order elections." *Electoral Studies* 30(4):689–699.

Somer-Topcu, Zeynep. 2009. "Timely decisions: The effects of past national elections on party policy change." *Journal of Politics* 71(1):238–248.

Somer-Topcu, Zeynep. 2015. "Everything to everyone: The electoral consequences of the broad-appeal strategy in Europe." *American Journal of Political Science* 59(4):841–854.

Somer-Topcu, Zeynep. 2017. "Agree or disagree: How do party leader changes affect the distribution of voters' perceptions." *Party Politics* 23(1):66–75.

Somer-Topcu, Zeynep and Margit Tavits. 2023. "Message distortion as a campaign strategy: Does rival party distortion of focal party position affect voters?" *Journal of Politics* 85(3):892–904.

Somer-Topcu, Zeynep, Patrick Fournier, and Ruth Dassonneville. 2025. "Personal issue importance effects on voters' perceptual accuracy of party issue positions." *Journal of Elections, Public Opinion and Parties*. FirstView.

Somer-Topcu, Zeynep, Margit Tavits, and Markus Baumann. 2020. "Does party rhetoric affect voter perceptions of party positions?" *Electoral Studies* 65:102153.

Soroka, Stuart N. and Christopher Wlezien. 2010. *Degrees of Democracy: Politics, public opinion, and policy*. Cambridge: Cambridge University Press.

Spoon, Jae-Jae and Jeffrey Nonnemacher. 2024. "Looking around the neighborhood: how subnational electoral politics affects voters' perceptions of parties' positions." *Journal of Elections, Public Opinion and Parties*. FirstView.

Sylvester, Christine, Zachary Greene, and Benedikt Ebing. 2022. "ParlEE plenary speeches data set: Annotated full-text of 21.6 million sentence-level plenary speeches of eight EU states. V2." Harvard Dataverse. https://doi.org/10.7910/DVN/ZY3RV7.

Tavits, Margit. 2005. "The development of stable party support: Electoral dynamics in post-communist Europe." *American Journal of Political Science* 49(2):283–298.

Tavits, Margit. 2007. "Principle vs. pragmatism: Policy shifts and political competition." *American Journal of Political Science* 51(1):151–165.

Tavits, Margit. 2008. "The role of parties' past behavior in coalition formation." *American Political Science Review* 102(4):495–507.

Tavits, Margit. 2013. *Post-communist Democracies and Party Organization*. Cambridge: Cambridge University Press.

Thies, Michael F. 2001. "Keeping tabs on partners: The logic of delegation in coalition governments." *American Journal of Political Science* 45(3):580–598.

Thomson, Robert, Terry Royed, Elin Naurin, Joaquín Artés, Rory Costello, Laurenz Ennser-Jedenastik, Mark Ferguson, Petia Kostadinova, Catherine Moury, François Pétry, and Katrin Praprotnik 2017. "The fulfillment of parties' election pledges: A comparative study on the impact of power sharing." *American Journal of Political Science* 61(3):527–542.

Tobin, James. 1958. "Estimation of relationships for limited dependent variables." *Econometrica: Journal of the Econometric Society* 26(1):24–36.

Tomz, Michael and Robert P Van Houweling. 2009. "The electoral implications of candidate ambiguity." *American Political Science Review* 103(1):83–98.

Tomz, M., J. Wittenberg and G. King. 2001. "CLARIFY: Software for interpreting and presenting statistical results, Version 2.0." http://gking.harvard.edu.

Tucker, Joshua A. 2006. *Regional Economic Voting: Russia, Poland, Hungary, Slovakia, and the Czech Republic, 1990–1999*. Cambridge: Cambridge University Press.

Van Der Velden, Mariken, Gijs Schumacher, and Barbara Vis. 2018. "Living in the past or living in the future? Analyzing parties' platform change in between elections, the Netherlands 1997–2014." *Political Communication* 35(3):393–412.

Volkens, Andrea, Pola Lehmann, Theres Matthieß, Nicolas Merz, Sven Regel, and Bernhard Weßels 2017. "The Manifesto Data Collection. Version 2017b." https://gking.harvard.edu/clarify.

Wagner, Markus and Thomas M. Meyer. 2023. "How do voters form perceptions of party positions?" *British Journal of Political Science* 53(4):1351–1362.

Walter, Barbara F. 1997. "The critical barrier to civil war settlement." *International Organization* 51(3):335–364.

Weeks, Ana Catalano, Bonnie M. Meguid, Miki Caul Kittilson, and Hilde Coffé. 2023. "When do Männerparteien elect women? Radical right populist parties and strategic descriptive representation." *American Political Science Review* 117(2):421–438.

Whitaker, Richard and Shane Martin. 2022. "Divide to conquer? Strategic parliamentary opposition and coalition government." *Party Politics* 28(6):999–1011.

Williams, Laron K. and David J. Brule. 2014. "Predictably unpredictable: The effects of conflict involvement on the error variance of vote models." *British Journal of Political Science* 44(2):287–299.

Williams, Laron K. and Guy D. Whitten. 2012. "But wait, there's more! Maximizing substantive inferences from TSCS models." *Journal of Politics* 74(3):685–693.

Zaller, John. 1992. *The Nature and Origins of Mass Opinion*. Cambridge: Cambridge University Press.

Zaller, John and Stanley Feldman. 1992. "A simple theory of the survey response: Answering questions versus revealing preferences." *American Journal of Political Science* 36(3):579–616.

Acknowledgments

The authors are very grateful to Jonathan Homola, Debra Leiter, and Zeynep Somer-Topcu and to the series editors Ray Duch, Anja Neundorf, and Randy Stevenson for wonderful feedback and advice on the manuscript. We also wish to thank Jim Adams, Heike Klüver, Jochen Müller, Diana O'Brien, Flori So, Jae Jae Spoon, Daniel Weitzel, and Simon Weschle for constructive conversation on the project's early stages. Finally, we are grateful for comments received on this project at University College London, Humboldt University, the 8th Annual Conference of the European Political Science Association, the 81st Annual Midwest Political Science Association Conference, the Asian Polmeth XII, and the 11th Conference of the Australian Society for Quantitative Political Science. Any errors of omission or commission belong to the authors alone.

Cambridge Elements

Comparative Political Behavior

Raymond Duch
University of Oxford

Raymond Duch is the co-founder and Director of the Centre for Experimental Social Sciences (CESS) at Nuffield College University of Oxford. He established and directed similar CESS centers in Chile, China, and India. He is also co-Director of the Candour Project that assembles a global team of research scholars with expertise in behavioral economics and data analytics addressing challenging health policy issues.

Anja Neundorf
University of Glasgow

Anja Neundorf is a Professor of Politics and Research Methods at the School of Social and Political Sciences at the University of Glasgow, UK. Before joining Glasgow, she held positions at the University of Nottingham (2013-2019) and Nuffield College, University of Oxford (2010-2012). She received her PhD from the University of Essex.

Randy Stevenson
Rice University

Randolph Stevenson is the Radoslav Tsanoff Professor of Public Affairs at Rice University in Houston, Texas. Professor Stevenson works and teaches in the areas of survey design, applied statistical methods, comparative mass political behavior, comparative political psychology, and experimental design.

About the Series

This Elements series is aimed at students and researchers interested in understanding how and why the political behaviour, perceptions, attitudes, emotional responses, interest, knowledge, and identities of citizens are conditioned on the political, social, and economic contexts in which they experience the political world.

Cambridge Elements

Comparative Political Behavior

Elements in the Series

Conspiracy Theories and their Believers: A Comparative Outlook
Daniel Stockemer and Jean-Nicolas Bordeleau

Mass Polarization across Time and Space
Isaac D. Mehlhaff

Voters' Perceptions of Party Brands
David Fortunato, Thiago N. Silva and Laron K. Williams

A full series listing is available at: www.cambridge.org/ECPB

For EU product safety concerns, contact us at Calle de José Abascal, 56–1°,
28003 Madrid, Spain or eugpsr@cambridge.org.

www.ingramcontent.com/pod-product-compliance
Lightning Source LLC
LaVergne TN
LVHW011850060526
838200LV00054B/4261